CONCILIUM
Theology in the Age of Renewal

CONCILIUM

Theology in the Age of Renewal

Volume 55: The Future of Marriage as Institution

THE FUTURE OF MARRIAGE
AS INSTITUTION

Edited by

Franz Böckle

Herder and Herder

1970
HERDER AND HERDER
232 Madison Avenue, New York 10016

CONTENTS

Editorial

TRADITIONAL forms of law and order are being widely questioned, and sexuality, with marriage as its institutionalized form, is no exception. Under the "new morality" slogan, a world-wide movement is afoot that seeks to reform sexual morals. An accusing finger is also pointed at traditional Christian morals. It is accused of being primarily responsible for the promotion of repressive moral norms which have not only limited the freedom of Church members but which in many parts of the world have also had a marked influence on the development of civil law. The charges are accompanied by demands which in part hark back to the gospels, but which through a dialectical process have emancipated themselves in the secular sphere. Thus we have a curious situation in which many of our contemporaries employ arguments against the traditional defence of marriage and its sexual norms that are Christian in origin.

The main objection is that for centuries Christian moral teaching has devalued sexuality and has tolerated it in marriage only as a means of conceiving children. Human sexuality as such has not been seen as a benefit of marriage, as the expression of love: the tendency has been to regard marriage as above sex and consequently to deny the connection between sexuality and love.

In fact, however, this "means to an end" way of thinking is *au fond* not so very different from the "means towards the satisfaction of desire" thinking to be found among some extreme representatives of the goodness of sexuality. These people, so the argument continues, are merely going to the other extreme:

7

sexuality is so important, it is said, that it can only impart personal fulfilment within indissoluble marriage. It is sexuality, not marriage, that is fundamental to man. One can no more seek the legitimization of sexuality in marriage than one can legitimize marriage merely as something required by sexuality. Sexuality, therefore, must be seen for what it is in itself and in terms of its particular importance for the human individual person. In this connection, the Church is suspected of defending indissoluble marriage as a legal institution not out of respect for human love but rather in an attempt to delimit human freedom.

So much for the charges laid against the Christian Churches.

The public discussion of these points, and the resultant pastoral situation, force us to review our own attitudes. Realization of the need for this gave rise to this issue of *Concilium*.

First, we consider the findings of modern Scripture studies. An exposition of the ethics of marriage and sex found in the Old Testament shows us a long cultural development that has many parallels with comparable cultures while also enjoying basic characteristics of its own on account of its connection with belief in Yahweh and the covenant relationship. The Bible seems to confirm what cultural sociology generally has described as "the formation of social systems instigated by religious thought forms" (A. Gehlen). God's salvific actions among men by no means exclude the natural laws of development but rather make use of them. One wonders, therefore, whether one is *obliged* to consider polygamy a consequence of the fall from an ideal paradisiacal state, as an expression of the emergence of sin? In any event, one cannot consider polygamy to have developed from a state of original monogamy; hardly either as a sinful sign of a promise not yet fulfilled. Neither may we take the "one flesh" reference as proof of a divinely established monogamous order. The two that become one, though in the singular, applies to all men and all women.

The New Testament contribution seeks to clarify the original meaning of what Jesus said about marriage. The author comes to the conclusion that though Jesus used legal language when speaking about divorce and separation, he made it "alien", "in order to break through the legal aspect in the interests of disclosing the reality of human relationships". Numerous Catholic exegetes nowadays argue this way. Jesus objected to the contemporary practice of separation, and promoted an awareness of principles that precede the law. His word is like the prophet's call and has the character of promise, in as far as it presents God's will as the possibility of faith. Precisely for this reason, what he says may not simply be taken at face value as law. It is not separable from the domain of faith.

With the death of Jesus, the early Church was faced with the difficult task of applying his teaching within the actual concrete situations of the believing communities. The need for established order quickly became clear. Quite a lot of space in this issue is given to a consideration of the development of the legal code that then began. Looking at history in this way preserves us from misleading absolutizations of traditional forms and structures, and opens up fresh possibilities of re-orientating current ecclesiastical practice. If the specifically salvation-historical and eschatological significance of Jesus' teaching is taken seriously, we are obliged to ask if we can take Jesus' radical demands without more ado as the basis for civil law in modern society. For civil law must realistically take into account man's "hardness of heart".

This issue also contains very instructive contributions on the development of Anglican and Reformed Church marriage theology. A similar article on modern movements within Catholic theology would have shown that the common return to biblical sources has brought about significant progress within the old argument about the sacramentality of marriage. The religious roots of marriage lie within marriage itself, in the agreement between the partners based on fidelity and love. In binding himself in fidelity to another, man acts in a supremely free manner. He will not be unaware of the demands such self-giving make on him; but it will be a step he takes in the light of his life's total meaning and of the freedom he possesses.

This call to live in conscious faith in God's strengthening grace mediated by Jesus Christ is a call to live marriage as sacrament. A man whom baptism has made a member of the Church and who in faith and conviction promises to love his partner for ever, expresses a love that in God's grace will bring salvation. Such a couple promote the Church as the bride of Christ: their promises to one another witness that in the Church Christ has irrevocably entrusted himself to mankind (as one who does so in marriage), and has made every aspect of human reality a means of salvation. This is all that is meant when Catholic theology refers to the sacramentality of marriage. The practical consequences of this theology are now being widely pondered.

FRANZ BÖCKLE
THEO BEEMER

PART I
ARTICLES

Josef Franz Thiel

The Institution of Marriage:
An Anthropological Perspective

THIS article is an attempt to examine some typical aspects of marriage from an anthropological viewpoint. It is not a detailed account of the various forms of marriage, but a treatment of factors which, according to anthropological research, determine the nature of marriage. In view of the limited space available, the number of pertinent questions, and the range of relevant ethnic groups, I shall for the most part limit myself to African experience. Nevertheless, in order to allow my comments an appropriately comparative basis, I shall make some reference to the Semitic peoples and the Tibetan nomads.

Anthropologists are acquainted with a variety of unions that have some affinity with marriage; they are recognized as wholly legitimate by the particular society. Nevertheless, although children may be born of such relationships, a decisive characteristic is absent: these unions do not determine the social status of the issue. For the purposes of this article, the only relationship admissible as marriage is that recognized by society as a lawful institution for purposes of legitimate descent. As far as is known, all peoples apply quite definite norms to marriage and propagation, and accordingly to the preservation and increase of human society. Even relatively non-authoritarian groups and those with a diffuse social structure, such as certain nomadic tribes, do not trust the maintenance of their ethnic group to impulse and chance. There is not and there certainly never has been such a thing as institutionalized promiscuity.

I. MARRIAGE AS A SOCIAL INSTITUTION

The anthropologist L. Mair defines African marriage as "an association between two persons for mutual support and the procreation and rearing of children". She qualifies this by remarking that "it usually has also the wider aspect of alliance between groups of kin".[1] This characteristic of African marriage also applies to marriage among most non-industrialized peoples. Marriage is primarily the concern not of the partners but of their parents, and most particularly of the elders of their lineage. Marriage is seen not as something absolutely new but as the means by which the family is extended. Therefore one may say that marriage is under the aegis of the family.

Among most peoples with an archaic social structure, the individual is not an end in himself but finds the meaningful basis of his existence in his community. Hence one speaks of a *corporate personality*. If an individual's egotistical behaviour causes him to be excluded from his lineage, he is simultaneously deprived of any content in his life. He is cut off from the stream of life transmitted through the elders. For most Africans exclusion from a lineage is equivalent to a sentence to death; it means a slow and shameful process of decay.

All members of a lineage trace their origin to a common ancestor or ancestress. They are organized in a homogeneous community, which forms an economic, social and religious whole to which both the dead and the living belong. The patriarch is at the head of the lineage. He often controls the common treasury, which supplies the bridewealth for a member's future wife. He also knows the groups with which for generations members of his lineage have been allowed to unite in marriage, and those which are forbidden.

The utmost solidarity is required within the lineage. Each member has to make the plans and concerns of the lineage his own. Everyone contributes to the bridewealth when a male marries; everyone receives a portion of the price when a female is given in marriage. When one of their lineage has married, the

---

[1] L. P. Mair, "African Marriage and Social Change", in *Survey of African Marriage and Family Life*, ed. Arthur Phillips (London, 1953), p. 4.

Yansi of Central Africa say, "*We* have taken a wife". If a child is born of this union, they declare, "*We* have received a child". It is reported that Ewondo-speaking women in the Cameroons say, "I am married with the Etenga", instead of stating that they are married to a particular individual.

This strict organization of the lineage is very important for a marriage, since in most cases the elders choose a partner for those ripe for marriage. Admittedly most ethnic groups do concede a free choice of partner to their young members, in the sense that they can refuse one they find disagreeable. But in most cases they hardly possess enough endurance and stubbornness to oppose their desires to the elders' will. Above all, this is true of girls, although it applies to boys too. In any case a free choice of partner is of much less moment to members of strongly traditional societies than to Europeans, for they think it only natural that the elders alone should have a say in the matter; the well-being of all members of the lineage is their concern, and therefore the arrangement of a marriage is their affair and not that of the young people. G. Hulstaert says of the Nkundo bride who does not find her intended bridegroom a pleasing choice: "But finally she bows to the paternal wish, preferring to enter into a union against her own desires rather than suffer the more or less serious displeasure of her family."[2] Henninger says of "freedom of espousal" among the Arabs:

> The more settled their domicile, the stricter are their conditions of ownership. Therefore, among the half-Bedouin (small livestock breeders) and those of fixed abode, the economic bonds of the family-group are firmer than among the full Bedouin (camel breeders), and much more stress is laid on the bride-price than among the latter. Because of the higher bride-price, divorce is more difficult and less frequently resorted to among the non-nomads than among the Bedouin. On the other hand, the high bride-price easily becomes an object of tribal speculation, and therefore tends to prevent freedom of choice in marriage, which is more prevalent among the full Bedouin.

Young women who refuse a suitor run the danger of receiving no more offers, since such a refusal is a disgrace for the prospective husband and his family. It is reported from Ruanda that for

[2] G. Hulstaert, *Le mariage des Nkundo* (Brussels, 1938), p. 113.

this reason girls usually accept the foremost tender, even when they find the young man disagreeable; their most ardent desire is to become a wife and mother, since only then will full membership of their society be available. Marriage pure and simple is the ideal to be sought after. Traditional African society does not know and attributes no value to the single way of life. Adults who will not marry count as social outsiders and easily come under suspicion of witchcraft. A girl who refuses several suitors is forcefully castigated by the Yansi: "Do you want to live without a man and bear no children? Why do you think God gave you breasts and what marks you as a woman? Certainly not just for looking at!" When the Yansi tell stories round the fire in the evening, they applaud the tale of the incredibly beautiful though haughty girl who rejected many suitors and in the end had to marry a python as her punishment.

II. The Purpose of Marriage

Marriage for love is not unknown among strongly traditional societies, but it is a relatively infrequent phenomenon. In general, it might be said that among them one marries first and then begins to fall in love, whereas in the Western world one falls in love first and marries after. I asked various young married people in the Congo whom they loved most. None of them named his or her marriage partner first, but chose instead parents or children. Often the husband or wife ranked after brothers and sisters. A Swazi riddle says: "If your mother and wife were drowning, whom would you save first?" The answer: "My mother. I can always get another wife but never another mother." An expert on African marriage writes: "Marriage often gives the impression of two individuals who have been simply brought together without anything fundamentally new having been created through their union."[3]

To have children must be considered the main purpose and even as the *conditio sine qua non* of marriage. If one partner is sterile and the other wants the marriage to be annulled, the elders must always approve divorce. If the wife is barren, the husband is always allowed another wife. Some African tribes

[3] J. Binet, *Le mariage en Afrique noire* (Paris, 1959), p. 41.

even make the new-wed bride's younger sister accompany her into marriage, so that she can "help out" if the wife proves to be unfruitful. It is also a practice among many tribes for a sterile man to have his wife impregnated by a friend, both to avoid the shame of childlessness and to have descendants, since as the husband he is the legal father of any children born.

Why is fertility so important for African peoples? Someone is a fully effective member of a tribe only if he has children. If he has none, he is denied legal succession to a political office or a position of honour in his group. The Yansi call an infertile woman *mur okwa*—a creature of death. Even if she is young and rich, she is without meaning for her society, and becomes a target of contempt. Even women and children may freely treat her as a public laughing-stock. Among the Okavango, sterile men are frequently compelled to commit suicide. Something of the depth of shame attached to sterility can be appreciated when one realizes that in Africa suicide occurs very rarely and only in absolute extremity.

Yet the main reason for the great significance of fertility is that descendants serve to perpetuate the family. By producing children one extends the work of one's ancestors and contributes to their continued life. Therefore, procreation has a virtually sacred character among these tribes. It is widely believed that the ancestors will finally die in the other world if the lineage dies out on earth. Those tribes who believe in re-birth also think that their ancestors are re-born in their descendants. The procreation of children therefore becomes an act of piety that a man owes to his community and his forebears. This attitude to children also means that most tribes will gladly accept children born out of wedlock, for they signify an increase of the mother's lineage. Abortion is infrequent among these peoples, even though abortifacients are known. M. Hermanns writes of the Tibetan nomads: "A pregnant girl will never have an abortion, for she is not put to shame by her condition. On the contrary, her fertility makes her more desirable as a future marriage-partner. The child born before marriage goes to her parents."

Marriage as a legal institution offers a lineage the possibility of further extension, even though the rules of the social structure may have condemned it to extinction. For example, among the patrilinear Lozi, if a man dies and leaves only daughters behind him, the eldest inherits his herd and "marries" wives in his name. These wives take lovers, and the dead man counts as the legal father of the children born. Among the matrilinear Yansi, a man whose lineage is threatened with extinction marries a slave. Since slaves have no lineage, the children belong to their father's group. It is reported of the Tibetan nomads that they will allow a girl to be married to the god of heaven. She is then permitted to receive lovers "honourably", and to bear children for her family.

III. MARRIAGE AS A PROCESS

Unlike European marriages, the African variety is not legalized in a few minutes. There is no one moment of time that can be accounted as deciding its full institutionalization. African marriages occur as a process over a long time, and often over several years. It is even arguable that marriage is not necessarily fixed ultimately by the birth of a child. Many tribes allow the couple to sleep together as soon as the bargaining over the bride-wealth has reached a certain stage and the bride's family has received certain gifts. But this stage of the proceedings does not yet determine the permanent lineage. A significant step towards realization of the marriage is made when the bride leaves her family and enters her husband's house, or when the man enters the woman's. This can be seen as the point when the marriage proper begins. But even in this phase the marriage is still under test. Only with the gradual payment of the bridewealth, the accompanying ceremonies, and the birth of children, is the bond gradually confirmed and a stable marriage thought to develop. Henninger says of the Arabs: "The actual marriage cannot be assigned to a particular moment, even though marriage is usually taken as consummated by reception into one or other community."

Occasionally a ceremony takes place when the wife leaves her group. The woman is withdrawn from the protection of her family spirits and put under that of her husband's. In so far as religious ceremonies take place in conjunction with the conclusion of a marriage in Africa, they have to do with the ancestor cult

and with magic. In Tibet, on the other hand, they are significant and devoted partly to honouring the guardian spirits of the
tent and the ancestors, and partly to honouring the god of heaven.
Among the Arabs, however, "Religious ceremonies in connection with marriage are either insignificantly developed or wholly
absent. The slaying of a sacrificial animal and the accompanying
blood rites, which cannot be of Islamic origin, point to a more
ancient source of these rituals." (J. Henninger)

In some regions of Africa the bride has to make a kind of
public confession before being received into the marriage home.
Before her parents or close relations she gives account of all the
men who have made love to her. But once she is placed under
the protection of her husband's guardian spirits, all extra-marital
sex is counted and punished as adultery. In general, only the
wife is bound to marital fidelity. Among several tribes of the
Kwango–Kasai border territory, the young married couple enter
into a blood pact during the marriage feast or soon afterwards.
This pact binds both partners to a monogamous marriage and
often to marital fidelity as well. A marriage involving a blood
pact is indissoluble; popular opinion holds that the union is so
firm that both partners will die on the same day. However, this
pact is only a sporadic phenomenon.[4]

Virginity until marriage is not demanded by most tribes:
"Some of the most competent philologists assure us that in most
Bantu languages there is no word for 'virgin'; this, however,
need not necessarily mean that the conception is strange to their
mind."[5] For instance, the Tutsi of Ruanda (the ruling tribe until
Congolese Independence) required the bride to be a virgin at
marriage. But they allowed their sons to have sexual relations
with the wives and daughters of the subject Hutu. If a Tutsi
bride was not found to be intact on the wedding night, the husband was entitled to send her back to her parents. Maquet writes
in this regard: "Virginity was prized higher than beauty and in-
dustriousness. This they defended by maintaining that virginity

[4] H. Hochegger, "Pactes de monogamie", in *Le mariage, la vie familiale
et l'éducation coutumière* (Bandundu, Congo, 1965), pp. 91–2.
[5] E. Torday, "The Principles of Bantu Marriage", in *Africa* (July 1929),
Vol. II, 3, pp. 255–6.

was the guarantee of fertility and a stable marriage."[6] Virginity, therefore, is held to be a good thing in so far as it is promise of a harmonious marriage. Similarly, the woman's adultery is considered bad because it injures the husband's right to the fertility of his wife. Hence Africans look upon adultery as a sin against the seventh commandment. "With regard to the concept of moral value among the Semites," writes Henninger, "sexual misdemeanour is viewed above all under the head of an injury to justice—an assault upon the rights of another man (the father of an unmarried girl, or the husband of a married woman). The sexual element as such is generally considered a matter of moral indifference."

In the marriage ceremonies of the peoples considered here, consent does not play the same role as in Western cultures. As I have pointed out, the consent of both families is more important than that of the prospective partners, who often express their readiness for marriage symbolically. Among the Yansi, the girl accepts a small gift from the boy; among the nomads of Tibet, the bride and groom together consume a piece of sacrificial meat; among the Tutsi, each spits a mixture of herbs and milk on to the other's head; elsewhere they drink from a barrel; and so on. To many peoples, a public acknowledgment of love for a bride would be thought a sign of stupidity.

The bridewealth has a more important role than consent. Its deeper significance has often been ignored by outsiders. It has been seen as a payment for the bride of the kind made for slaves. Since the man enjoyed a privileged position in his society, it seemed that his wife could be properly designated his slave. Hence bride-price marriages in South Africa were considered to be transactions in which the husband bought his wife. In reality the bridewealth does not buy the woman, but compensates her family for the loss of her fertility. For instance, if the marriage is annulled and the wife has borne no children, the bride-price must be returned in full. But if the wife has had children, the husband receives nothing. The matrilinear Yansi say, "His bridewealth is returned to him in his children".

In earlier times the bridewealth did not have any economic

[6] J. Maquet, *Le système des relations sociales dans le Ruanda ancien* (Tervuren, 1954), p. 85.

value. Among cattle breeders it consisted of several head of cattle; but no economic use was made of them, inasmuch as they usually became the bridewealth for the young woman's "brother". Therefore brothers could often marry only after their sisters, and the cattle went the same way as the bride. Among non-cattle breeding tribes, copper rings, iron rods, spearheads, axes, cowrie shells and alcoholic drinks could serve as bridewealth. But most of these objects had no economic value apart from their function as a bride-price. Exchange marriages are common among the pygmies; if a group surrenders a marriageable girl, at a given time it will receive a marriageable girl from the man's group.

It is customary for the bridewealth to be paid in instalments. Earnest-money has to be paid before the bride is handed over, otherwise her family will not release her. The payment of the full sum can take years, but must be completed if the father finally wants to marry off his daughter and receive the money. Otherwise the price goes to his wife's family.

Whenever a part of the bridewealth is paid and whenever a child is born, certain ceremonies and festivities take place that draw the bonds of matrimony closer. Evans-Pritchard says of marriage among the Nuer: "The new social ties of conjugality and affinity are made stronger by each payment and by each ceremony, so that a marriage which is insecure at the beginning of the negotiations becomes surer with every new payment and rite.... Therefore a marriage which has reached the final rites may be regarded as a stable union and will generally prove to be so."[7] In addition, if the wife is peaceable and diligent the elders will not readily agree to a divorce. Such a marriage may be seen as virtually indissoluble.

The marriages of young people may be characterized as "living together", whereas those of older people may be called "life together". The latter are frequently exemplary unions of love. An old Yansi woman once bemoaned her husband's death thus:

Now I am alone and am without a man. When I come back from the fields in the evening the house is empty; he is no longer there waiting for me, waiting to greet me. When I wake up at night, I am alone in the bed. When I go out in the morning, he no longer

[7] E. E. Evans-Pritchard, *Kinship and Marriage among the Nuer* (Oxford, 1951), p. 59.

sees me on my way. I prepare the meal, but I must eat alone. He is no longer here; he has gone to another village and has left me alone.

I never heard young people offer so touching an expression of married love.

IV. Divorce

As far as is known, all the ethnic groups mentioned in this article permit divorce for certain weighty reasons. One such ground is the sterility of one or other partner. Opinions differ as to whether such a separation ought to be called divorce or the recognition of the non-fulfilment of a contract because an essential clause has been broken. Since marriage is a process extending over a certain length of time, and a bond which grows closer, it may be asked from what point it is possible to speak of actual divorce.

Although divorce is fundamentally possible with all tribes, it occurs relatively seldom in many groups. It seems to be less frequent among patrilinear than among matrilinear groups. The size of the bridewealth paid is less significant in this case, since it depends on the general prosperity or poverty of the group. Where the levirate and sororate are frequently met with, divorce would seem to be infrequent, because these institutions relate the woman closely to the husband's lineage. The divorce rate depends on the attitude of the particular society to marriage. If its ideal is a stable marriage (which can equally well be based on social, economic and moral grounds) divorce is seldom met with.

In general, a man marries for life. Above all, this applies to his first marriage. Children do not make divorce difficult because they would be a trouble to look after, but because their presence signifies that an essential clause of the marriage contract has been fulfilled. Some grounds commonly accepted as permitting a divorce are: repeated adultery by the woman; a chronic sickness that makes married life impossible; witchcraft that injures a marriage partner; gross dereliction of duty to the partner and children; and so on.

Like the contracting of marriage, divorce is a long process. Usually the wife leaves her husband for an undetermined length of time and goes to live with her family. The parents or the elders usually try to persuade the couple to live together again. If the same difficulties recur, and force the couple finally to separate, the elders proclaim a divorce. Like the contracting of marriage, divorce is a concern of the lineage. Political power has nothing to do with it. But often village elders who enjoy a reputation for knowledge of the law are drawn into the negotiations. Divorce ceremonies, where they exist, are usually simple. Among the Yansi they take the form of a withdrawal of the wife from her husband's guardian spirits, and her return to those of her family.

V. Summary

Among the ethnic groups examined in this article, the individual exists not for his own sake but wholly for the sake of his kinship group. Marriage is not only his personal concern but above all that of his group. Free choice of a partner is not excluded but is not of primary importance for the individual. Marriage serves essentially to produce legal descendants, in order to ensure the perpetuation of the particular lineage. At the same time, it offers the possibility of establishing friendly relations with other groups.

Contrary to Western practice, the contracting of marriage is a lengthy process among the peoples mentioned here; it can take years. Only in the course of time does it become a stable institution. The bridewealth does not buy the bride but compensates for the loss of her fertility. Consent plays a subordinate role in marriage ceremonies. It can be expressed symbolically, and be wholly absent. It is important that the elders of both families should approve the union and thereby give it a legal character. In Africa the religious ceremonies are mainly a matter of the ancestor cult. Marriage is sacred in so far as it extends the work of the ancestors and guarantees their continued life. The ancestors are not ordinary dead people, but extra-natural and powerful beings who exert considerable influence on the course of earthly life. Among the Tibetan nomads, not only are ceremonies held in honour of the ancestors but prayers, dedications and sacrifices,

partly addressed to the god of heaven, impart a religious character to the contracting of marriage. Divorce and polygyny are
practised by almost all people; but for the most part the latter is
the ideal form of marriage and therefore the kind to be sought
after.

Translated by John Griffiths

Eugene Hillman

The Development of
Christian Marriage Structures

THE following reflections are grounded on some data provided by history and by anthropology. These data are necessarily limited by the space allotted for this article; and they are selected because they seem representative enough for the purpose of dramatizing in a concise manner the general situation as regards both the development of Christian marriage structures, and the lack of such development, in the course of the Church's missionary encounter with the culturally diverse peoples of the world. The current debates, consequent upon the recent re-thinking about the ends of marriage and the present social pressures in certain societies, are not discussed here explicitly; because the significance of these debates, which have perhaps consumed more theological attention than they really deserve, is already widely appreciated. But the following reflections could still have some relevance to these debates, at least among those whose theories on marriage have not yet become universal absolutes.

I. THE NON-WESTERN WORLD

The development of the theology and structures of Christian marriage in the Western world, although periodically arrested, is discernible; and this on-going process has been outlined by contemporary scholars.[1] It is, however, still difficult to say very much

[1] Cf. J. E. Kerns, *The Theology of Marriage* (New York, 1964); E. Schillebeeckx, *Marriage: Secular Reality and Saving Mystery*, Vol. II (London, 1965).

about such a development in areas under the influence of non-Western cultures during the past few hundred years of the Church's missionary history. Practically speaking, there has been none. At least there has been no ostensible movement of a positive kind. And certainly there has been nothing comparable to the evangelical-cultural symbiosis that occurred during the course of the Church's earlier missionary engagement with the peoples of Europe. The reasons for this later stagnation are not hard to find.

In spite of an abundance of lip-service that has been officially paid to the principles of respect for, and adaptation to, the diverse ways of men and their various socio-economic institutions and cultural patterns, missionaries really have not been permitted, and most of them were not even inclined, to apply these principles.[2] Instead, Christianity—neatly wrapped up with selected and dated ethnic conventions—has been simply exported to the non-Western world, like a "package deal", to be accepted or rejected exactly as it is presented; or with only those slight modifications that might be permitted by a small group of ecclesiastical careerists who mount guard over the Christian message as though it were the private property of a particular segment of humanity. In general this has been the situation since the mid-eighteenth century when the Roman Curia, in the name of Pope Benedict XIV, officially put an end to the radically incarnational missionary approach that had been initiated by Robert de Nobili in India, and by Matteo Ricci in China.[3] Since then the practices of the Church in Italy have generally been regarded as normative for the rest of the world.

Even today, in spite of all the fine principles enunciated by the Fathers of Vatican II (on the respect due to the immemorial cultural practices of different peoples: the need for careful study,

[2] Cf., for example, the instructions of Pope Gregory the Great, to missionaries in Britain, 18 July 601, in Bede, *Ecclesiastical History of the English Nation*, Bk. 1 : 30; also the instruction of Sacred Congr. Prop. Fide to missionaries in 1695, in *Collect. Prop. Fide* (Rome, 1907), Vol. I, p. 42; and the missionary encyclical letters of the last five popes.

[3] Cf. J. L. McKenzie, *The Power and the Wisdom* (Milwaukee, 1965), p. 247: "Historians now generally agree that if the Roman Curia had permitted the Gospel to be preached in China in the eighteenth century with certain adaptations to Chinese culture, the country would have become substantially Catholic." See also A. Toynbee, *Civilization on Trial* (London, 1946), p. 85.

adequate information and sympathetic understanding, before making any judgments), we can still point to some astonishingly uncritical, and highly official, statements which betray both a lack of information and a failure of understanding. Indeed, it seems that Western cultural arrogance is congenital, however unconsciously it may be expressed. We are perhaps justly indicted by the African writer who recently remarked "that the West has always had a pejorative attitude towards Africa", and this is "self-evident".[4] This problem, with its profound implications for the theology of marriage, may be illustrated by focusing our attention first on some different cultural appreciations of polygamy; and then, more briefly, on the fact of different cultural understandings of matrimonial consent.

The writers of the Pastoral Constitution on *The Church in the Modern World* have, for example, rather obtusely consigned polygamy (without even bothering to distinguish its various forms) to the same category as "the plague of divorce, so-called free love, and other disfigurements" that obscure the excellence of marriage.[5] They might have done well to have first studied the meaning of this custom, and the far-reaching reasons for it, as presented by such writers as Jomo Kenyatta.[6] At least they might have consulted some modern manual of anthropology.[7]

A curious lack of information, and perhaps a measure of wishful thinking, is discernible also in the encyclical letter of Pope Paul VI, addressed to the peoples of Africa in October 1967. Here we read that "even the system of polygamy, widespread in pre-Christian and non-Christian societies, is no longer linked, as it was in the past, with the social structure today; and fortunately it is no longer in harmony with the prevailing attitude of African peoples".[8]

A factual consideration of the real situation hardly justifies such a sanguine outlook. Relatively few African countries have enacted legislation against traditional polygamy; and in some of

[4] Joseph O. Okpaku, "Let's Dare to be African", in *Africa Report*, Vol. 13, No. 7, Oct. 1968, p. 13.
[5] *Gaudium et Spes*, n. 47.
[6] J. Kenyatta, *Facing Mount Kenya* (London, 1956).
[7] For example, L. J. Luzbetak, *The Church and Cultures* (Techny, 1963).
[8] Paul VI, *Africae Terrarum* (Oct. 1967), n. 33; English translation in *African Ecclesiastical Review*, Vol. 10, No. 1 (Jan. 1968), p. 81.

these countries, Mali for example, the new marriage codes represent an "ingenious compromise" with customary laws.[9] The problems of enforcing a new law of monogamy are formidable in any
society where traditional plural marriage is intimately bound up
with the kinship system, the norms of land tenure, inheritance
regulations, economic security, social control, notions of prestige,
family continuity, and so on. It must be remembered that the
populations of sub-Saharan Africa are still predominantly rural;
and that, for economic reasons, they will have to remain so in the
foreseeable future.[10] This means that traditional social institutions
and cultural values still profoundly influence the lives of most
people. The thinking of the relatively small educated *élites*, however well articulated and widely publicized, does not yet reflect
the thinking of the uneducated masses; and in most of these countries the rate of formal education (and the new attitudes which
follow therefrom) is not keeping pace with the population in-
creases. There are other reasons why the traditional patterns must
still be taken seriously: for example, some seventy-five per cent
of the people are neither Muslims nor Christians.[11]

Moreover, all the available data on the extent to which polygamy is practised in this part of the world, as well as the first-
hand experience of countless missionaries, suggests that "the
prevailing attitude of African peoples", at least with respect to
marriage structures, has not changed much during the past forty
or fifty years.[12] Among some peoples this practice has become much
less common than it was previously, while among others it has

[9] Cf. J. W. Salacuse, "Developments in African Law", in *Africa Report*,
Vol. 13, No. 3 (March 1968), pp. 39 ff.
[10] Cf. René Dumont, *False Start in Africa* (London, 1966) (*L'Afrique
Noire est Mal Partie* [Paris, 1962]).
[11] Cf. John V. Taylor, *The Primal Vision* (London, 1965), pp. 28-9, 112.
[12] Cf. E. Hillman, "Polygyny Reconsidered" in *Concilium*, March 1968
(American edn, Vol. 33); Economic Commission for Africa, Workshop on
Urban Problems: The Role of Women in Urban Development, "Polygamy
—The Family and the Urban Phenomenon", United Nations Economic
and Social Council (Mimeographed), 25 July 1963; International African
Institute—London, *Social Implications of Industrialization & Urbanization
in Africa South of the Sahara* (UNESCO, Paris, 1956); David B. Barrett,
Schism and Renewal in Africa (Nairobi, 1968), p. 241: "It is clear also
that polygamous society will not disappear for some time to come. ... In
the 580 tribes who so accept it (78 per cent of all tribes south of the
Sahara), the polygamous past will certainly be defended strongly. ...

become far more common; and this even in urban areas. Among many other reasons, this may be due to the fact that, where general monogamy has replaced *simultaneous* polygyny there tends to be a notable increase in prostitution, casual concubinage, adultery, divorce, illegitimate children, *consecutive* polygyny and *consecutive* polyandry.

Now, according to the most recent sociological data, the general situation in sub-Saharan Africa is something like this.[13] Among the majority of peoples polygamy (which almost always means simultaneous polygyny in this part of the world) is a traditionally and economically sanctioned institution which is normal and general. In thirty-four per cent of these societies the incidence of polygyny amounts to more than twenty per cent; while it is common (although restricted to certain types) in another forty-four per cent of these societies. In the remaining twenty-two per cent this form of plural marriage is either very limited or non-existent.

This, of course, is not an exclusively African custom, as missionaries in some other parts of the world know very well: New Guinea and Papua, for example. Nor is this the only non-Western custom that deserves far more positive reflection than has so far been given by Christian theologians.[14] Polygamy just happens to provide a particularly dramatic example of the Church's failure to take adequate account of the complex realities of family life, and the meaning of marriage structures, outside the walls of ancient Christendom.

The realization of matrimonial consent, to cite just one more example, among many peoples seems hardly compatible with the Roman legal conception of achieving an irrevocable *consensus* at one precise moment in the course of the formal nuptial rite. Like the whole reality of marriage itself, valid *consensus* is understood by many only in terms of gradual growth. Ideals and aspirations

---

Hence we can see that in those societies where the institution is or has been common, this factor will continue to be present as a powerful component of the zeitgeist."

[13] This general picture is provided by Barrett, *op. cit.*, p. 116.

[14] For some other examples, see Ralph E. S. Tanner, *Transition in African Beliefs* (Maryknoll, 1967); and J. V. Taylor, *op. cit.*, pp. 109–11: some peoples believe that marriage is consummated by nothing less than childbirth.

are not realized in a moment. In many societies authentic *con-sensus*, both socially and psychologically, is achieved only through a series of customary actions, involving more people than merely the two who are immediately concerned, over a long period of time, normally before the formal ceremony of marriage, and sometimes after as well. Usually it is not at all clear at what point exactly, if there is a precise point, the mutual consent is actually realized. But, without all of these customary stages, many people find it hard to accept the authenticity of the marriage union. Such misgivings, although not articulated philosophically nor even juridically, are no support for the stability of a marriage which has to be lived, after all, in that particular cultural context, not in ancient Rome.

II. The Western World

A truly incarnational approach to other cultures had been common enough in former times: during the period of the Church's missionary expansion among the peoples of the West. It could not have been otherwise in the beginning. The apostles, in their efforts to make the Christian message intelligible and relevant among the nations, could not have invented new socio-cultural forms any more than they could have invented a new language. There is no universal Christian culture, and every human act is conditioned by a particular culture. So, to start with, all social structures and institutions are culturally limited and basically pre-Christian, just as all men are—all of us. It is well known that these first missionaries, and quite a few since then, saw the direct imposition of foreign forms as a stumbling-block to the acceptance of their message. On this very issue Paul with-stood Cephas to his face (cf. Gal. 2. 11–14), and the apostolic council in Jerusalem took a positively liberal stand during this first great crisis of survival in the Church (cf. Acts 15. 1–29).

Indeed, the whole Pauline conception of an authentically uni-versal people of God is best understood as a missionary's total theological response to the Judaizers who would bind Christianity with their archaic ethnic conventions.[15] At Pentecost the Church was sent into the whole world for a ministry of reconciliation, to

[15] Cf. J. L. McKenzie, *op. cit.*, p. 202.

take on the flesh of one new people after another, so that Christ might become manifestly "the same Lord of all" (Rom. 8. 12), by taking unto himself, in a "wonderful exchange",[16] all the cultural "riches of the nations" (cf. Ps. 2. 8; 47. 8 f.; 72. 10 f.; Isa. 60. 5–11; Matt. 2. 11; Apoc. 21. 25 f.). Against the Westernizers, who have long since replaced the Judaizers, it is still necessary to reaffirm vigorously the Church's original ecumenical purpose. The choice is still the same: universalism or ethnocentrism.

Through a gradual process, which was sometimes fully incarnational and sometimes merely symbiotic, Western cultural practices naturally shaped the structure of Christian marriage, even as these practices were themselves being influenced by the Christian message. "Thus down to the end of the fifth century in the West marriages were still celebrated in Christian families with some of the forms customary in pagan times, and the nuptial rite prescribed by Pope Nicholas I in the ninth century was that in use in imperial Rome with the substitution of the Mass for the pagan sacrifice."[17] The use of the ring, for example, as a symbol of betrothal, and later as a sign of the contract, comes directly from pre-Christian Roman practice.[18] From this same source comes also the Church's official formulation of the purposes of marriage: "in order to bring forth children".[19]

Roman law, inspired directly by the traditional pagan "religion of the hearth", provided the structure for both indissolubility and monogamy,[20] as well as various norms for determining the validity of Christian marriages: for example, the impediments arising from impotence, consanguinity, affinity and disparity of cult.[21] The comprehensive nature of this early pagan influence may perhaps be summarized thus:

[16] Cf. Vatican II, *Ad Gentes*, nn. 11, 22; *Lumen Gentium*, nn. 13, 16; *Gaudium et Spes*, nn. 44, 45, 58.

[17] K. S. Latourette, *A History of the Expansion of Christianity*, Vol. I (New York, 1937), p. 326.

[18] Cf. J. Carcopino, *Daily Life in Ancient Rome* (Harmondsworth, 1964), p. 94.

[19] Cf. W. M. Lawson, "Roman Law: A Source of Canonical Marriage Legislation", in *Resonance*, No. 4 (Spring 1967), p. 9; E. Schillebeeckx, *op. cit.*, p. 15.

[20] Cf. E. Schillebeeckx, *op. cit.*, p. 7.

[21] Cf. W. M. Lawson, *loc. cit.*, pp. 10 ff.

According to the evidence of a contemporary letter, the *Epistula ad Diognetem*, Christian marriage was much the same as that of the pagans. As a general rule, Christians were bound to conform in this and in similar matters to the pattern of life of their own environment. The synod of Elvira, held around the year 306 . . . , also accepted as its point of departure that the marriages of baptized Christians were celebrated like those of unbaptized pagans. The Church simply accepted the subjection of her members to the Roman legislature. . . . In Catholic communities, marriages concluded according to the prevailing social customs were considered to be valid. . . . As far as pagan ceremonies were concerned, the clergy was only intent to point out that Christians should refrain from sacrifices, and, although they might rejoice in their celebrations, they were bound to avoid all pagan excesses.[22]

It is not surprising, therefore, that "Canon Law's basic principles and obligations of the marriage contract seem to be similar to, if not identical with, Roman Law".[23]

But it is no longer possible to pretend that pagan Roman customs and laws are universally relevant. The fact that these things were "baptized" cannot mean that they are now universally constitutive elements in Christian marriage, although legions of missionaries have been taught to act as though this were the case, and as though non-Western marriage customs were somehow less appropriate for Christians. Even "when Christianity spread to the Germanic tribes, it was some time before the Church succeeded in getting her marriage theory of *consensus*, based on Roman law, accepted".[24] In this particular cultural situation "marriage was seen as a contract between two tribes or extended family groups, rather than a contract between the bride and the bridegroom themselves".[25] Yet the marriage customs of the different tribes were "strictly observed with the aim of preventing any later doubts or disputes" over the validity even of Christian marriages.[26] The stability of marriage and family life was then considered more important than external conformity to foreign concepts and laws.

[22] Schillebeeckx, *op. cit.*, pp. 18 f., 20, 21 f.
[23] Lawson, *loc. cit.*, p. 9.   [24] Schillebeeckx, *op. cit.*, p. 33.
[25] *Ibid.*, pp. 33 f.   [26] *Ibid.*, p. 36.

In those days the official Church went very far in its concern for the evangelization of Western peoples. The following statement, astonishing as it may be, is taken from a papal letter addressed to a missionary in northern Europe:

> Gregory, the servant of the servants of God, to Boniface, our most holy brother and colleague in the episcopate. . . . Since you seek our advice on matters dealing with ecclesiastical discipline, we will state with all the authority of apostolic tradition what you must hold, though we speak not from our own insufficiency but relying on the grace of him who opens the mouths of the dumb. . . . As to what a man shall do if his wife is unable through illness to allow him his marital rights, it would be better if he remained apart and practised continence. But since this is practicable only in the case of men of high ideals, the best course if he is unable to remain continent would be for him to marry. Nevertheless, he should continue to support the woman who is sick, unless she has contracted the disease through her own fault. . . . This, my dear brother, is all that need be said with the authority of the Apostolic See.[27]

Thus, under certain conditions, papal permission was actually given for the practice of a particular form of simultaneous polygyny. This concession seemed reasonable enough in the Germanic missionary situation. As Tacitus had noted, polygamy was customary among some of these northern "barbarians".[28] And an old moral principle, enunciated by St Augustine in his *Reply to Faustus*, could very well have been invoked: ". . . A plurality of wives was no crime when it was the custom; and it is a crime now because it is no longer the custom." Augustine's argument was that the practice of polygamy becomes wrong when it is no longer customary; because, then, it arises only from an "excess of lust". We know also, from a number of existing documents, that Pope Clement VII came very close to granting this same concession to King Henry VIII; and at least one prominent theologian

[27] Quoted by Adrian Hastings, "An Encyclical from Pope Gregory II", in *The Tablet*, Vol. 222, No. 6689 (3 August 1968), p. 764: Letter of Pope Gregory II, 22 November 726, to Boniface, missionary bishop in Germany; from C. H. Talbot, ed., *Anglo-Saxon Missionaries in Germany* (London, 1954), pp. 80–3.

[28] Cf. Manas Buthelezi, "Polygyny in the Light of the New Testament", in *Africa Theological Journal*, No. 2 (February 1969), p. 68.

at that time, "apparently Cardinal Cajetan, thought that this was indeed within the papal power".[29]

As Western culture changed, so did the theology of marriage. There is, for example, a striking difference between the teaching of Pope Gregory the Great that conjugal intercourse always involves sin, and the teaching of Pope Pius XII that there is nothing wrong in seeking and enjoying this pleasure.[30] These irreconcilable views can be explained only in terms of cultural conditioning. If Gregory's theology could be so determined by the ethos of his particular time and place in history, then we may assume that all theology is apt to be so determined. "The changes in what Christian writers say from the second to the twentieth century reflect nothing so much as a struggle between two cultural views of human sexuality, with the Christian view gradually prevailing."[31]

Now we know, of course, that there are many more cultural views of human sexuality and conjugal union; and if so many centuries were required in the West before "the Christian view" finally prevailed, then why should we expect similar developments, indeed profound changes, to be effected more rapidly— even as a precondition for baptism—in the non-Western world? The conception of marriage, and the customs associated with this institution, are central in any cultural complex; they represent such deep emotions, such tenaciously held convictions, such detailed social structures, and so many generations of careful deliberation, that the consequences of immediate change, imposed from the outside, are apt to have very disconcerting repercussions both socially and psychologically.

This kind of reflection on history and anthropology might suggest also that the ideal of Christian marriage, as set forth by a number of modern Western writers, just may not be at all the last word on the subject. If long and wide human experience is any kind of a teacher, then it is possible that much more could be learned about marriage and family life from the practices and institutions of non-Western peoples. Most of the married inhabitants of the world do not, after all, live in the West; nor are

---

[29] Cf. E. C. Messenger, *Two in One Flesh: The Mystery of Sex and Marriage*, Vol. II (London & Glasgow, 1948), pp. 113, 159–61.
[30] Cf. J. E. Kerns, *op. cit.*, pp. 61, 79.   [31] Kerns, *op. cit.*, p. 90.

they, in terms of authentic human experience, any less contemporary than the minority who happen to live in the West. So, again, some care must be taken by the builders of universal Christian theories.

Thus we must see the currently popular Western conception of marriage—usually presented in terms of enduring emotional love and mutually fulfilling inter-personal relationships—as the product of a particular historico-cultural experience.[32] This ideal is not widely appreciated elsewhere in the world; nor was it much appreciated even in the West just a few generations ago, outside certain very limited social circles. Pragmatically, anyway, it is not at all certain that this late Western conception is either a necessary or an adequate basis for the stability of a life-long commitment. This necessity or adequacy might be rather difficult to prove against the growing divorce rates in the same culture areas. So, for the moment at least, this development should be treated with some reservation. Discernible developments, within the framework of the social-evolution hypothesis, are not in every case progressive; and we must also keep in mind the problematical nature of any progress-measurements that are obtained by the use of our own locally manufactured criteria.[33]

In connection with this same point, just one final remark may be appropriate; and this with reference to the place of "bringing forth children". The arguments used by Christians in affluent Western societies, in favour of limiting the number of births, become crassly dishonest and even hypocritical when dramatic references are made to the starving children in India.

III. The Privilege of the Faith

At first glance it might appear that the various canonical regulations, known generally as the "privilege of the faith", represent a true development of Christian marriage structures as a result of the Church's missionary enterprise during the past few hundred years; at least since the publication, in 1537, of the

---

[32] Cf. Anthony Levi, "Moral Teaching and its Evolution", in *The Tablet,* Vol. 221, No. 6655 (9 December 1967), p. 1279.

[33] Cf. Werner Bröker, "Aspects of Evolution", in *Concilium,* June 1967 (American edn., Vol. 26).

Constitution *Altitudo* by Pope Paul III. This is allegedly based upon, and sometimes confused with, the so-called "Pauline privilege" (cf. 1 Cor. 7. 10–15); and it was progressively extended through its application to missionary problems, especially the problem of the simultaneous polygynist who wished subsequently to become a Christian.[34] Originally, however, the "privilege of the faith" appears to have been a more general principle based, somewhat tenuously perhaps, on the Petrine power to bind and to loose. In fourth-century Spain, for example, this principle was used to justify restrictions against Jews: against their taking Christian wives, keeping Christian slaves, and holding authority over Christian groups.[35]

The regulations set forth in *Altitudo,* and in the subsequent papal documents which gradually extended the scope of this "privilege", meant in effect that the Pope authorized the dissolution of marriages previously recognized as valid; and this was done "in favour of the faith" of the would-be Christian spouse who was then free to marry again. What these regulations amount to, in modern language, is real divorce and remarriage. What is clearly permitted, under a variety of conditions, is *consecutive* polygyny and *consecutive* polyandry. What seems never permissible, whether "in favour of the faith" or for the "salvation of souls", is *simultaneous* polygamy; and perhaps only because this had been forbidden by Roman law which profoundly conditioned the historical interpretations of the New Testament teaching about marriage.

In any case, these canonical regulations were not at all sympathetic towards the specifically non-Western socio-economic institutions of plural marriage which were somehow considered less suitable for Christians than the Western forms of plural marriage. So the Church did succeed in bringing about a measure of external conformity with the Western, and especially Roman, understanding and pattern of marriage. As many missionaries know, the cost of this conformity in terms of human anxiety and alienation has been considerable.

This is not to say that the "privilege of the faith" regulations

[34] Cf. Paul E. Demuth, "The Nature and Origin of the Privilege of the Faith", in *Resonance*, No. 4 (Spring 1967), pp. 60–73.
[35] *Ibid.,* pp. 63 ff.

were ill-inspired. Doubtless they were motivated by a keen desire for the "salvation of souls"—especially the souls of husbands—at a time when it was commonly believed that salvation was practically impossible for those who did not belong visibly to the Church. The method used was exceedingly juridical; and the Christian concern for the rights and the destinies of the wives who were "sent away" was not much in evidence. But the regulations do signify an earnest effort to meet some of the real and perplexing problems that arise from the pristine commitment of the Church: to summon Christ's disciples from among all peoples. The solutions found possible in the past are not necessarily the only possible solutions. An equally innovating effort by theologians today, basing themselves, however, on rather different cultural premises, could still lead the Church towards a more fully Christion solution to these same problems which have not yet vanished.

CONCLUSION

By way of conclusion it might suffice to say that a lofty ideal of Christian marriage, as found in the New Testament, should be held up as a goal to be striven after. But, considering what human life is like in the real world, and with due respect to the vast diversities of culture, the actual realization of this normative ideal by all married Christians in every historico-cultural situation can hardly be expected. And this actual realization certainly should not be regarded as a precondition for active participation in the sacramental life of the new people of God. Nor should we continue to imagine that striving after this ideal somehow involves the imposition, with an immediate and total acceptance, of one particular cultural conception and pattern of marriage. Just as there is no universal Christian language, so there is no universal Christian culture. To pretend otherwise is to place a stumbling-block before the pilgrim people, called from among all nations, who can reach their goal only step by step in the course of generations.

The pilgrimage is hard enough as it is, without the addition of excess cultural baggage on the backs of men: "heavy and oppressive burdens" (cf. Matt. 23. 4 f.). The forbearance of the official Church in other matters—the social institutions of slavery, war and economic exploitation—should give us pause. Do we "traverse sea and land" (Matt. 23. 15) with a liberating message that summons Christ's disciples from among the nations, and then make their last condition worse than the first?

Pierre Grelot

The Institution of Marriage: Its Evolution in the Old Testament

IT IS not possible to provide here a complete theological consideration of marriage as an institution; to do this it would be necessary
to refer to the whole of the Bible. In this article I intend merely
to see whether revelation exerted a real influence on a cultural
phenomenon Israel inherited from its ancestors. From this I go
on to consider whether as an institution marriage was subject to
an evolutionary process which reached its final stage in the New
Testament. Three points need to be dealt with: (1) Legal: how
did the law affecting marriage evolve into its final form in the
Torah? (2) Theological: how did ideas regarding marriage develop in Genesis and the prophets? (3) How, from this twofold
viewpoint, did Jewish marriage become stabilized in post-exilic
Judaism continuing down to the beginnings of the present era?

In an investigation of this kind special attention must be paid
to the economic and social conditions in which the Jewish family
took shape during its long history; account must also be taken
of the cultural environment forming its background and against
which it stood out in startling originality. But more especially
we must consider the religious factor and its influence on the
evolution of marriage in Judaism. The limits of the present article
do not allow fuller treatment of the subject. Even the references
to the learned works showing the development of these three
stages will be kept to a minimum: every reader knows that a
simple reference to a book of the Bible is at the same time an
invitation to consult the relevant commentaries.[1]

[1] The following important works, relevant to this article, are listed here:

I. From the Common Law of the East to the Rules of the Torah

1. The Common Law of the Patriarchal Period

The family as it appears in ancient biblical tradition is of the patriarchal type. At the first stage of this period (Abraham and Isaac) the best Eastern parallels are to be found in the Code of Hammurabi (c. 1700) and in the contracts of Nuzi (fifteenth century), that is, in that Mesopotamian milieu from which Abraham's tribe originated. Abraham and Isaac had only one wife in the formal sense of the term. In the same way, in the Code of Hammurabi, a man is not allowed to take a second wife unless the first is sterile. And he loses even this right if his legitimate wife provides him with a slave as concubine for the purpose of ensuring legal descendants; this happened in Abraham's case. Sarah gave him Hagar as his concubine (Gen. 16. 1–2). The husband retains the right to take a second concubine; thus Abraham took Keturah (Gen. 25. 1–5), and his brother Nahor also had a wife and a concubine (Gen. 22. 20–4). In the next period, Jacob had two wives who each gave him a concubine to increase their descendants (Gen. 29. 15–30, 24), and Esau had three wives (Gen. 26. 34; 28. 9). A somewhat similar development can be found in the collection of Assyrian laws towards the end of the second millennium.[2]

The importance accorded to the wife's fertility, and to descendants in the masculine line who would ensure the continuance of the tribe and the handing on of the inheritance, explains these legal provisions: the family comes before the individual and must continue through him. At a later period, Psalm 27. 3–5 reminds us

---

R. de Vaux, *Les Institutions de l'Ancien Testament* (Paris, 1958), pp. 37–65 (contains a bibliography); R. Patai, *Sex and Family in the Bible and the Middle East* (New York, 1959); J. Pedersen, *Israel: Its Life and Culture* (Copenhagen, 1926), I, pp. 29–96; H. Ringeling "Die biblische Begründung der Monogamie", in *Zeitsch. f. Ev. Ethik* (1966), pp. 81–102; cf. *Theol. des A.T.s*, by W. E. Eichdrodt and G. von Rad.

[2] The translation of the Code of Hammurabi and the Assyrian laws can be found in J. B. Pritchard, *Ancient Near Eastern Texts Relating to the Old Testament* (Princeton, 1950), pp. 153 ff. and pp. 180 ff. For the Assyrian laws, see the recent commentary by G. Cardascia, *Les Lois assyriennes*, Littératures anciennes du Proche Orient (Paris, 1969), pp. 63–71.

that the strength of the family depends on the number of its male members. The custom of levirate marriage provided for the extreme in cases in which the husband died without issue: it was a sacred duty for his brothers and nearest relatives to produce a child for him (cf. Gen. 38. 6–10). The needs met by polygamy are clear, though some passages of the Bible make no effort to hide the difficulties that could arise from it (thus the rivalry between Sarah and Hagar: Gen. 16. 3–6; 21. 8–14); but the good of the tribe is more important than these lesser difficulties. A further consequence is a sexual ethic in which men and women are placed on different levels; wives and concubines have certain well-defined rights, but the husband retains a wide freedom of action; no one reproached Judah for sleeping with Tamar, although he mistook her for a prostitute (Gen. 38. 15–18). Further, only the man could take the initiative in connection with marriage: the wife was the subject of a contract between her future husband and her father or, if the latter were dead, his successor as head of the family (Gen. 24. 58 f.). The whole affair was arranged between families, and the husband bore the significant title of *ba'al*, "owner". A woman who was a slave clearly could not refuse the position of concubine that was offered her.

2. *Written Law in the Pentateuch*

The various codifications of Mosaic law are based on this common law and form adaptations of it to a society in evolution. Three points should be noted here: impediments to marriage, polygamy and divorce. On the first point, the two lists of prohibitions in Leviticus (18. 6–23 and 20. 9–21) reflect the requirements of religious law towards the end of the monarchy. It is possible to argue about the reasons for the prohibition of incest in primitive societies—Levi-Strauss attributes it to the need to exchange women between families (*The Basic Structure of Kinship*, 1968). Here this reason has practically disappeared from view. In a society in which endogamy remains a traditional ideal, it is a question of protecting the nearest relationships: it would be shameful for a man to "uncover the nakedness" of his mother, sister, daughter, his maternal or paternal aunt, his daughter-in-law, two sisters at the same time.... At an earlier period Moses' father, nevertheless, had married his aunt (Ex. 6. 20) and Abraham his father's sister (Gen. 20. 12); even in David's time this degree of relationship did not constitute an impediment (see 2 Sam. 13. 13). Thus the law had developed in a restrictive sense as society evolved and grew more complex. In the matter of polygamy the written legislation is somewhat vague. The Book of the Covenant (Ex. 21. 7–8) only mentions the case of the daughter sold as a slave by her father in order to enumerate her rights (21. 10 f.) and the conditions under which she may be bought back (21. 8). Nothing is said about official wives. On the other hand, at the time of the judges an ordinary landowner could have two (1 Sam. 1. 2), and an important chieftain like Gideon must have had a large number of wives and concubines (cf. Jgs. 9. 2–5). But at the time of the kings, the royal harem seems to have grown as time went on, either to ensure the power of the royal house (cf. 2 Kgs. 10), or to satisfy the king's pleasures (cf. 1 Kgs. 11. 2–3). In this context, the problem of foreign wives was most acute at the specifically religious level: it is to be observed in the case of Solomon (1 Kgs. 5–8) and of Ahab (1 Kgs. 18. 4; 19. 14). Here Deuteronomy, while it seems to endorse simultaneous bigamy (21. 15–17), and union with women captured in war (21. 10–14), reacts strongly against royal polygamy (17. 17). Actually, economic factors certainly confined practices of this kind to a small number of men—landed proprietors, civilian and military members of the aristocracy. Polygamy tended to accentuate the difference between social classes at a time when Amos was inveighing against the upper classes of Samaria (Am. 4. 1–3), and Isaiah against those of Jerusalem (Is. 3. 16–24). The ideal of the patriarchal family was a long way off.

The only legislation in Deuteronomy about divorce (24. 1–4) concerns the prohibition against taking back a repudiated wife who has remarried; the reasons justifying divorce are left rather vague. The ultimate effect of this legislation is to regulate customs that were common throughout the ancient East, thus giving the Israelites a system adapted on the one hand to their economic and social organization and, on the other, to the fundamental imperatives of faith in the one God to whom Israel belonged in a special manner. The tradition of the two moralities, one for men and the other for women, is firmly maintained. For example, a man may be accused of adultery only if he encroaches on the rights of another man (Deut. 22. 22; Lev. 20. 10). Defence of marriage as an institution is dealt with from the social point of view rather than from that of sexual morality. The idea of marriage as an agreement reached between two equal partners on the basis of their mutual love seems to have no place, even if, in practice, love could play a part; this was so particularly among the poor, whose monogamous marriage was the usual rule. Positive law is not the consequence of an ideal principle derived from revelation; it provides the framework for an actual situation determined by the culture of the times.

II. THEOLOGICAL CONSIDERATION OF MARRIAGE

1. Theology of the Creation

In all the pagan civilizations of antiquity the sacredness of sex, love and marriage found expression in myths of a very similar structure: the myth of the father-god, generally Uranian, and of the mother-goddess, the personification of the earth (except in Egypt, where relationship of the sexes is reversed). There is the myth of the goddess of love: Innina or Ishtar in Mesopotamia, Astarte in Canaan, Aphrodite among the Greeks and Venus for the Latin world. Divine Forces immanent in the Cosmos were in charge in every instance of the use of the genital powers. In addition, to ensure the fertility of men, beasts and the earth, sexual rites were practised in the temple of the goddess of love: sacred prostitution was held to possess a special value as imitative magic. On this point the monotheism of the Israelites at the outset effected a radical break with the traditions of neighbouring peoples. Yahweh had neither wife nor son; consequently sexual rites were forbidden and severely put down (see Deut. 23. 19 f.; 2 Kgs. 23. 7). From this particular point of view it is possible to talk of a real demythologization and desacralization of sexuality and everything connected with it. But revelation was to place the sacred character of marriage and fertility on a different basis by linking them with the plan of God the Creator.[3]

[3] In addition to the *Théologies de l'Ancien Testament* and the commentaries on Genesis, see P. Grelot, *Le Couple humain dans l'Ecriture* (Paris, [2]1964), pp. 15–57 (cf. pp. 131–9); English edition, *Man and Wife in Scripture* (London, 1964—translation of first edition).

The "Yahwist" account of the creation (Gen. 2, probably tenth century) makes no claim to provide a definite theory of the primitive monogamy of the human race on a par with archaic societies. On the contrary, Genesis 3, by showing that sin made its appearance in history right from the first use of human freedom, excludes the possibility of ever connecting an "original" state of humanity unmarked by the relative domination of Evil, both as regards social institutions and the individual conscience. But *before* this beginning of history the narrator endows God's creative act with a paradisiacal setting, belonging to the language of myth, enabling him to outline an ideal view of God's plan for the human race. This plan remains subjacent to the development of the world, as an end directing it which will be achieved at the conclusion of time; as we know, eschatology assumed in the prophets the characteristics of Paradise regained. It is from this particular point of view that the author, though writing in an environment where polygamy, concubinage, divorce, and so on, were legally admitted, showed mankind called into existence in the form of a pair (Gen. 2. 18–24), corresponding, moreover, to the physical reality of sexual union. Woman is for man "bone from his bones and flesh from his flesh"; and so he acknowledges her as the "helpmate found for him".

Can this aetiological account, which shows woman as man's complement, be quoted as evidence of a monogamous tendency in the author? By no means, answers H. Ringeling, who cites in the contrary sense the practice of polygamy which forms the context of the narrative.[4] Two facts are in opposition to this view. On the positive side, the conclusion of the passage in Genesis (2. 24) emphasizes three points: man "joins himself to his wife", a phrase which denotes both family affection (Rt. 1. 14; 2. 23) and sexual love (Gen. 34. 3); he "leaves his father and mother" to affirm in some way the pair's autonomy; he and his wife "become one flesh", fleshly union being the sign of an association in which the whole being is committed. But this is only the ideal in paradise, for the negative counter-proof follows. On the one hand, the coming of sin into the world, shown as the human

[4] *Art. cit.*, note 1, p. 87.

pair's tragedy (Gen. 3), results in the degradation of the inter-personal relationship which takes the form of greed and domina-tion (Gen. 3. 16 f.). On the other hand, the appearance of a new cultural phenomenon makes its mark on the history of sinful humanity: Lamech, Cain's descendant, institutes polygamy (Gen. 4. 19–24). This was the situation then prevailing. Israelite legis-lation was to adapt itself to it, but there was a certain gap between this situation and the Creator's fundamental plan which persists throughout the history of Israel.

With the priestly historian (Gen. 1. 27 f.) the inter-personal re-lationship between the sexes is much less marked. It is seen ex-clusively from the point of view of fertility which is regarded as the essential sign of God's blessing. Mythical or ritual sacraliza-tion is entirely set aside and the creative Word of God forms the basis of the whole value of carnal love. Here the writer shares the preoccupations of the ancient family law in which polygamy was regarded as licit. Yet on the one hand the account of the creation does not allude to it; on the other, in the story of the flood Noah and his sons still have only one wife (Gen. 6. 18)—as if polygamy was introduced only at a later date, during some cultural de-velopment tarnished by sin. Of course, we must not read too much into these passages from Genesis 1 and 2. They do not mention when or how the original ideal was to be restored, nor even if it could be for the lack of any eschatological outlook. Was the eschatology of the prophets to provide the necessary complement?

2. The Symbolism of the Couple in the Prophets

In the eschatology of the prophets the human couple is re-garded from the different point of view of its symbolic meaning. This is not, of course, in relation to the divine realities but to the fundamental institution on which the religion of Israel is based, namely, the covenant between God and his people. This theme is introduced by Hosea with reference to his own experience of marriage (Hos. 1 and 3) explained in a long speech as a real parable in action (Hos. 2. 4–25). His marrying a "wife of prosti-tution" who gave him "children of prostitution" is interpreted as the first symbolic action representing the position of Yahweh taking Israel for his people.

The continuation of the story is not clear. The following at least can be made out from it: on God's orders the prophet "still loves" the adulterous wife who perhaps had been repudiated and in any case had fallen into the power of another; he buys her back and takes her again as his wife (Hos. 2). The meaning of the symbol is obvious; it portrays the love of God as redemptive love. This second action of the prophets is still more paradoxical than the first: according to the law and customs of those days no husband would have acted like this. But it is in this way that God proposes to act. The covenant had been broken by Israel's adultery (2. 4) but God still pursues the faithless wife with his love; after some experience of misfortune causing her to be sorry for her former way of life (2. 9b), he will charm her and take her away to the wilderness and speak to her heart (2. 18); the whole incident concludes with a fresh betrothal in an atmosphere of paradise regained (2. 21–22).

All through this tragic love story, there can be discerned the appearance of a new dimension of conjugal love itself, a personalization of the bond between the man and the woman which goes beyond the old view of fertility and the continuance of the family. Not, of course, within the setting of the old covenant and its law, but in the new situation which at the end of time will also assume the form of a covenant to reveal in its fullness the redemptive love of God.

After Hosea, the symbol recurs in several of the prophetic books with some slight differences due to the legal arrangements then in force—the legislation, that is, concerning adulterous wives in Jeremiah 3. 1 and Ezekiel 16. 38–40; the possibility of bigamy in Jeremiah 3. 6–10 and Ezekiel 23, mentioned to recall the similar position of Samaria in relation to the divine Bridegroom. But when we look to the future we find that these secondary features disappear: Jerusalem becomes the only bride of Yahweh and the other cities become her daughters to take part in the eschatological wedding feast (Ez. 16. 53–63). God's redemptive love achieves the astonishing miracle of the reconciliation of the outraged Bridegroom with the "wife of his youth" whom he was unable to bring himself to forget (Is. 54. 6). By thus displaying to believers the ideal couple formed by the God-Bridegroom and the Community-Bride (Is. 54; 61. 1–6) all these passages so filled with hope surely influenced religious thought indirectly by incorporating in it an image placed by the accounts of the creation outside historical time. Set between a primitive paradise which is definitively lost and a paradise regained (which will be a return to the beginning), the human state is to be understood according to a dynamic viewpoint from which no reality can be excluded. Why, therefore, should marriage be left out of account?

III. Marriage and Family in Post-Exilic Judaism

1. *The Ideal of Marriage in the Prophets and Wisdom Literature*

After the Exile, the expectation of eschatological salvation was the continual burden of Jewish thoughts and hopes. At the practical level, economic and social evolution caused considerable changes in the matter of the family. It may be wondered, indeed, if a similarly careful reading of Genesis 1–2 and the prophets would not influence it laterally though without changing its legal foundations. In actual fact, at about the time when Nehemiah and Ezra reacted forcefully against the marriage of Jews with foreign women (Nem. 13. 23–28; cf. 10. 1–31; Ez. 9. 1–15), the prophet Malachi, while supporting the legal requirement in accordance with Deuteronomy (Mal. 2. 10–13), adopts a new attitude to divorce: God stands as witness between the man and "the wife of his youth"; the man is not to break faith with her "for Yahweh hates divorce" (Mal. 2. 14–16). This statement puts forward an ideal but it does not possess force of law; two centuries later Ben Sirach was still advising men to get rid of an intractable wife (Sir. 25. 26). In Wisdom literature, in addition to praise of virtuous wives, which could be understood even among those practising polygamy, a significant emphasis can be noticed on faithfulness to the wife "of youth" (Prov. 5. 15–19; 5. 1–23; Sir. 26. 13–18) and on the extolling of chastity, even going so far as to include desires and looks (Job. 31. 1 and 7–12). In all these passages there is no allusion to polygamy. Job himself, whose way of life was that of the ancient patriarchs, had only one wife (Job 2. 9). Judith, also, in her widowhood remained faithful to her dead husband (Jdt. 8. 2–8; 16. 25). The inter-personal aspect of the conjugal relationship had certainly made considerable progress in men's minds.

This new ideal of marriage is given its best expression in the book of Tobit (third century?). Tobit's and Sarah's marriage was of course the result of a special disposition of divine providence: in this way God heard the twofold prayer of the elder Tobit, and of Sarah the ill-starred bride. Nowhere in the story is there any allusion to broken marriages; thus we cannot tell what the writer thought of the positive law of divorce. He is in favour of the traditional endogamy (3. 17; 4. 12 f.; 6. 16; 7. 10 f.). But although he studiously copies the marriage stories in Genesis he makes no allusion to a plurality of wives, as if the question did not even arise in his case. His idea of the ideal and obviously monogamous marriage has its roots in the two accounts of creation, as is shown by the young couple's prayer on the night of their wedding day (Tob. 8. 6 f.). A clear allusion to Genesis 1 (use of the verb *create*) is combined with a paraphrase of Genesis 2. 18. Thus the two images of the original pair provided by Scripture are placed one on the other to constitute the ideal of Jewish marriage. Emphasis is given both to the perpetuation of the family, mutual help by husband and wife, and chastity in the use of marriage (cf. the addition in the old Latin version to Tob. 6. 16–22). In the absence of any allusion to the prophetic symbolism of the pair, there is in the book an ideal of conjugal morality which forms an excellent connection between the two. And so the song concluding the whole book glorifies the eschatological Jerusalem in terms repeating the passages in which she was shown as the Bride redeemed by her God (Tob. 13. 9–17; cf. Is. 54 and 60–62). It is hardly surprising that at a later date in St Paul the "mystery" contained in Genesis 2. 24 is compared to the relationship between Christ and his Church, revealing at the same time the definitive ideal of marriage (Eph. 5. 25–32).

2. *The Evolution of Customs*

There was, of course, a time lag between this expression of the ideal, antecedent to the time of salvation, and the juridical regulation of the institution of marriage still based on the law of Moses. With Ezra, the Torah was fixed on the basis of the old laws, without modification. This text was to constitute in the future the unchangeable framework of the law, the "tradition of the ancients" coming in only as the basis of jurisprudence. Yet a certain evolution can be detected. At the beginning of our era, Flavius Josephus makes explicit mention of Herod the Great's polygamy (*Jewish Antiquities*, 17, 13) and we find John the Baptist chiding Antipas for marrying his brother's wife (Mk. 6. 17). But the conduct of this royal family, and even that of the Hasmonean high priests, could not be taken as examples of Jewish family life at that time. Although the rabbinical legal literature provides for the possibility of polygamy, it was certainly something exceptional, even among the moneyed classes. The Tannait literature and the gospels "presuppose a society that was practically monogamous", for "the great mass of the population were to all intents and purposes monogamous".[5] In theory, the halacha of the Pharisees kept, nevertheless, to the rules laid down by Scripture. The discussions in it about divorce were concerned only with the reasons which made it licit. In practice, things could be different. From the fifth century, in the marriage contracts exchanged between the Jews of Elephantine, there can be found the possibility of divorce on the wife's initiative and even clauses formally forbidding polygamy. But this may have been due to a cultural influence coming from foreign sources, particularly the clause regarding monogamy.

In any case a still more remarkable evolution may be observed among the small Jewish group known as the Essenes. The *Damascus Document* (the *Zadokite Documents*) inveighing against the sect's enemies—that is, probably, against the Hasmonean high priests—formally prohibits bigamy, and also, no doubt, remarriage after divorce, on the authority of Genesis 1. 27 and 7. 9 (col. IV, 20–21 and V, 1). Similarly, extending to men the rule laid down by Leviticus, it forbids a man to marry his niece (col. V, 7–11). This restrictive halacha reveals a tendency which at the time of Jesus was certainly to be found only among a minority. But it is of interest to notice that Jesus' dictum on divorce (Mk. 10. 6 and parallel passages) is based on one of the texts to which the *Damascus Document* appeals (Gen. 1. 27 and 2. 24). This is not so fortuitous as may appear; we have already seen the importance of Genesis 1–2 in the development of the ideal of the family as advocated by the book of Tobit;

[5] G. F. Moore, *Judaism in the First Centuries of the Christian Era* (Cambridge, Mass., 1927), II, p. 122.

Jesus led to its conclusion a movement that had begun to take shape before his time.

This investigation can end at that point. It has shown on the one hand the relationship of marriage with a cultural element in course of evolution and, on the other, the dynamic quality of a revelation with implications of eschatological salvation which gradually manifested two traits. These were its connection with the wider institution of the family and its essence as the interpersonal relationship between man and woman.

Translated by Lancelot Sheppard

Paul Hoffmann

Jesus' Saying about Divorce and its Interpretation in the New Testament Tradition

THIS is an exegetical essay.[1] Its first part is concerned with determining what is the most primitive form of Jesus' saying about divorce that has been handed down to us, and what assertions that saying contains. A second part considers how Jesus' words, with the demands they make, were expounded in the various situations of the Early Church. And thirdly, the different points which have been made will be gathered together and related to the basic matter in question.

I. JESUS' SAYING ABOUT DIVORCE

In both the Q source of sayings (Lk. 16. 18 parallel Mt. 5. 32) and in the Gospel of Mark (Mk. 10. 11), a saying is handed down in which Jesus designates the divorce of one's wife as adultery. Literary-critical comparison of the various traditions leads to the

[1] The following more recent works contain further bibliographical material to which reference can be made for information on the numerous points of exegetical detail.—H. Baltensweiler, *Die Ehe im Neuen Testament* (Zürich–Stuttgart, 1967); G. Delling, "Das Logion Mk. 10. 11 (und seine Adwandlungen) im Neuen Testament", in *Nov. Test.*, 1 (1956), pp. 263-74; H. Greeven, "Zu den Aussagen des Neuen Testaments über die Ehe", in *Zeitschrift für evang. Ethik*, 1 (1957), pp. 109-25; H. Greeben, J. Ratzinger, R. Schackenburg, H. D. Wendland, *Theologie der Ehe* (Regensburg–Göttingen, 1969); F. Hauck, S. Schulz, Art. πόρνη κτλ, in *Theol. Dict. of the N. T.*, VI, pp. 579-95; R. Pesch, "Die neutestamentliche Weisung für die Ehe", in *Bibel u. Leben*, 9 (1968), pp. 208-21; A. Sand, "Die Unzuchtsklausel in Mt. 5. 31, 32 und 19. 3-9", in *Münch Theol. Zeitschrift*, 20 (1969), pp. 118-29; K. H. Schelkle, "Ehe u. Ehelosigkeit

conclusion that the Lucan version of the Q source[2] renders faithfully the original wording of the saying: "Every one who divorces his wife and marries another commits adultery, and he who marries a woman divorced (from her husband—Lucan addition) commits adultery."

A consideration of Mark 10. 11 shows that the oldest tradition is preserved first and foremost in Luke 16. 18a. For Mark quotes a saying whose wording is very like that of Luke 16. 18a, but which is, from a literary point of view, not dependent on the Q source of sayings. This double line of tradition enables us to establish the original wording of the saying with a high degree of probability.[3]

Jesus presupposes all that the Jewish Law has to say about divorce *and* adultery.[4] This Law is patriarchal and polygamous. Only the man has the right to divorce his wife. A woman can only in exceptional cases, and indirectly, bring about her own divorce. And the legal grounds for divorcing one's wife were disputed. The school of Schammai allowed it only in the case of unchastity, but according to the school of Hillel it was in the end a question purely for the husband's discretion. A woman is, through divorce, made free to marry again. The polygamous concept of marriage made for a double standard when it came to judging adultery too. For a married woman, any sexual relationship with a second man was regarded as adultery. But a husband who had sexual relations with another woman was not

---

im Neuen Testament", in *Wissenschaft und Weisheit*, 29 (1966), pp. 1–15. For the older exegetical discussion cf. A. Ott, *Die Auslegung der neutestamentlichen Texts über die Ehescheidung* (Münster, 1911).

[2] Mt. 5. 32a was edited by Matthew; v. 32b essentially confirms the wording of Lk. 16. 18b. Cf. below II, 3.

[3] H. Baltensweiler, *op. cit.*, p. 62, considers "and marries another" to be a casuistical addition from Q. In that case Lk. 16. 18b would also have to be struck out as secondary because it presupposes remarriage. Against this there is the fact that the predicate ("commits adultery") taken at its face value presupposes divorce and remarriage. Besides, the "addition" in no way detracts from the original assertion, for to the Jews divorce and remarriage go together.

[4] P. Billerbeck, *Kommentar zum Neuen Testament aus Talmud und Midrasch* (Munich, ⁴1965), I, pp. 303 ff., II, pp. 372 ff. (re marriage and divorce); I, pp. 294 ff. (re adultery).

answerable to his own wife for the same offence: he committed adultery only if he violated the rights of another man.[5]

Jesus, then, designates as adultery (and therefore illegitimate) an action which in Jewish Law was legitimate—the divorcing of a woman by her husband and his remarriage, or the marrying of a lawfully divorced woman. His provocative statement would have made two things clear to his listeners:[6] (i) marriage unites man and wife in a way that cannot be dissolved by the Law; (ii) a man can be answerable to his own wife as an adulterer (v. 18a)—the obligations of a woman to her husband, formerly *one-sided*, are now *mutual*. Man and wife are shown to be equal partners with equal rights.

Should we, then, think of this saying of Jesus as a law? To understand it, we must compare it with other sayings in which he shows his attitude to the Law. If we do this, we see that his words here are no more a law than is his condemnation of anger (Mt. 5. 21 f.), or of oath-taking (Mt. 5. 33, 34a, 37; cf. Jas. 5. 12), or of committing adultery in one's heart (Mt. 5. 27 f.). In these instances he does indeed use the language of the Law, but he does so in a way that alienates it from its customary legal use and breaks through the plane of law into that of reality. He reveals the reality of a human relationship in which God lays direct claim to man's response. And he frees this relationship from the strait-jacket of the Law. His statement on divorce must also be understood in this sense. Jesus criticizes the Law and lays bare the reality of marriage which, though subject to the Law, can never be adequately protected by it. His words contain a demand and a promise: he shows how great are the obligations human beings can assume with regard to each other, but also the chance of fulfilment which is offered them. So his saying is the norm and the criterion for any Christian answer to the question of divorce. It is *not law*, for it goes to the heart of the *reality* of marriage.[7] And it is clear from the history of Christianity that it

[5] We find a similar conception in the Hellenic-Roman world, cf. F. Hauck, *Theol. Dict. of the N.T.*, IV, 732 f.
[6] Re the following interpretation cf. P. Hoffmann, "Die bessere Gerechtigkeit. Auslegung der Bergpredigt III", in *Bibel und Leben*, 10 (1969), pp. 175–89.
[7] Cf. G. Bornkamm, *Jesus of Nazareth* (New York, 1960), pp. 96–100.

needed a great deal of explanation. We turn now to the first phase of that history.

II. The Interpretation of the Saying in the New Testament Tradition

We shall deal in three separate sections with the treatment of the saying in Mark, Matthew and Paul. It is no longer possible to find out how it was understood in the Q source, which represents early Palestinian Christianity, for its context there is not known. But a comparison with other variations in Q justifies us in supposing that it was taken literally:[8] for the Christian, divorce and remarriage are forbidden. Luke (16. 18) understood the saying as an ethical directive. Connected as it is with 16. 16 f., it illustrates his fundamental thesis that the demands of the Old Testament Law (16. 17) continue to hold good even in the era of the Gospel (16. 16). He may have chosen the saying on divorce as an example of the strict conception of marriage he wanted to present to his community as the centre-point of Christian ethics, in opposition to the unbridled sexual liberty in the heathen world around them (cf. Acts 24. 25 and Lk. 8. 14 on this point).

1. Mark 10. 1–12

In 10. 1–32 Mark has himself arranged in a catechetical manner the three traditional pieces about divorce, children and riches. Following on the announcement of the Passion and the words about discipleship, they set forth the demands Jesus makes in the situation of the Marcan community. And in the editorial fashion so typical of him,[9] Mark has attached the instruction given in the house to the disciples onto the dispute about divorce (10. 1–9). He has done so in order to crystallize Jesus' "teaching" for his community, by means of the saying on divorce.

H. Baltensweiler[10] has recently tried to re-establish the thesis

[8] Just as, e.g., Lk. 11. 42a is made into a rule of conduct by the Q addition of 42b.

[9] Cf. Mk. 4. 10–13, 34; 7. 17; 9. 28 f., 33; 13, 3 f.

[10] Op. cit., pp. 51–3. R. Schnackenburg, op. cit., p. 13, thinks v. 9 at least should be treated as an "original Jesus-word". For the history cf. R. Bultmann, Geschichte der Synoptischen Tradition (Göttingen, ⁴1961), pp. 25 f.

that the dispute about divorce relates something that occurred historically. But the very question which introduces the debate is a point against this thesis. A Jew, for whom divorce was something taken for granted, could scarcely have asked such a question. The way it is put, and the debate itself built up, show rather that the passage has from the very first been composed as a basis for Jesus' magisterial reply. Besides, the quotation from Genesis 2. 24 follows the Septuagint word for word; and it is from this quotation that the statement "and the *two* shall become one flesh" is taken, while the Hebrew text reads only "*they* shall become one flesh". And this Greek reading is a constitutive element of Jesus' reply. So it is highly probable that the dispute, together with Jesus' answer, only took on the form it has in Mark when it was received into the Greek-speaking Judaeo-Christian community.

As in the dispute about defilement and purification (Mk. 7), so here too the new order which Jesus' teaching opens up to men stands in contrast with the old Jewish order.[11] Divorce had been *commanded* by Moses (v. 4a, 5 as opposed to v. 4b) in a way that served only to show the obduracy and hard-heartedness of the Jews (cf. Mk. 7. 6). In opposition to this, Jesus reveals an order that has in fact been valid since the very moment of creation (v. 6–9). ἕνεκεν τούτου ("For this reason"—Trans.) (v. 7), which in Genesis 2. 24 refers to the creation of woman out of man, here refers back to v. 6: the creation of human kind as man and woman (Gen. 1. 27) is the foundation for the unity of marriage. But it is the last part of the quotation that is stressed: "and the two shall become one flesh", with the immediate repetition interpreting these words, "so they are no longer two but one". This combination of quotations has the effect of grounding the *unity* of marriage in God's act of creation itself; and v. 9 draws as a conclusion the principle: "What God has joined together[12] let not man put asunder". There is no question here of divorce or

[11] Cf. R. Hummel, *Die Auseinandersetzung zwischen Kirche und Judentum im Matthäusevangelium* (Munich, 1963), pp. 53 f., and the relevant places in the commentaries on Mark, especially E. Schweizer, *Das Evangelium nach Markus* (Göttingen, 1968), pp. 114–17.

[12] "God grounds not only marriage as such, but each and every marriage", W. Grundmann, *Das Evangelium nach Markus* (Berlin, ²1959), p. 204.

remarriage; rather, because the unity of each and every marriage is forged by God, even "separation" is regarded as an interference in God's work, an intervention that is in principle illicit for man.

The various statements of this "dispute" pericope have been composed with an aim which is primarily theological and christological. The Christian community is, with the help of Genesis 1, 2,[13] defending the "essence" and "demands" of marriage as revealed by Jesus, against the old order of the Jewish Law. Mark draws out the conclusions for the community in a house scene he has added on to the dispute. Here the disciples ask Jesus the meaning of what he has taught—Mark is hinting that Jesus' revelation is only accessible to the believer. For Jesus' reply Mark uses the saying that has also come down to us in Q (cf. I above), though here it must be read in connection with its new context. Thus it is noticeable that from v. 9 onwards not only divorce but also remarriage is in question. Both divorce *and remarriage* are forbidden for the Christian. The principle of v. 9 seems to have been qualified here as a result of the community's actual experience.[14] Verse 12 proceeds to widen the scope of the saying to accord with Hellenic-Roman law:[15] the wife is, in her turn, forbidden to divorce her husband and remarry. This broadening of the question shows two things: the saying was taken as a commandment to be fulfilled literally; and precisely for this reason it had to be brought into line with the new circumstances of Christian life.

2. *Matthew 19. 3–9; 5. 31 f.*

There are two main problems to be dealt with here: Matthew's particular redaction of the tradition, and the meaning of the so-called unchastity clauses. We shall begin with an analysis of Matthew 19. 3–9.[16] A comparison with Mark 10. 2 shows up the

---

[13] For the contemporary understanding of the Genesis passages cf. Baltensweiler, *op. cit.*, pp. 54–9 (with references to other literature).

[14] The theological reflection of the dispute-pericope is applied to the concrete ruling of v. 11 by the addition "(commits adultery) against her". The second marriage is adultery because the marriage bond to the first wife, which is God's handiwork, remains as before.

[15] For Hellenic-Roman marriage law cf. H. Conzelmann, *Der erste Brief an die Korinther* (Göttingen, 1969), p. 145, note 22 (refs. to literature).

[16] Besides the commentaries cf. R. Hummel, *op. cit.*, pp. 49–51; G.

new way in which the Pharisees' question is put. They ask: "Is it lawful to divorce one's wife *for any cause?*" And the whole composition of the dispute diverges considerably from the form it has in Mark 10. Jesus' reply points immediately to God's creative will (Gen. 1, 2), from which he deduces the irrevocable unity of marriage. God is expressly referred to as the creator (v. 4), and the quotation from Genesis 2. 24 is put in his mouth (v. 5). These changes were made in order to stress the fact that God's will is visible in the created order of life. The Pharisees argue against Jesus, pointing to the Mosaic *commandment* of divorce (v. 7, diverging from Mk. 10. 4). He parries their objection by interpreting Deuteronomy 24. 1 f. as a *concession* (v. 8a, diverging from Mk. 10. 4a, 5) which is contrary to God's original intention: "but from the beginning it was not so" (v. 8b, a Matthean addition). This alteration puts the Torah prescription on divorce into perspective against the wider-reaching order of creation: the commandment of divorce is only a concession which, as such, points back to the created order as the criterion by which it should be interpreted. Diverging again from Mark, Matthew joins the divorce-saying (Mk. 10. 11) directly onto the dispute (v. 9), and thus makes it the answer to the Pharisees' opening question. Jesus gives here, as he does in Matthew 15. 20b or 12. 12b, a lesson on the Law. His new, authoritative exposition ("And I say to you . . .") stands in opposition to the Jewish one, and can appeal for its justification to God's creative will itself. So in Matthew the dispute (19. 4–18) has a theological and hermeneutic function: the original created order is shown to be the criterion for interpreting the Law, and Jesus' interpretation with the directive it contains is thus shown to be the better exposition of God's will.

Verse 9 is a Christian Halacha, and in order to understand it we must first see how the unchastity clause added at this point into the saying should be interpreted. There is nowadays no longer any need to discuss the fact that the expressions μὴ ἐπὶ πορνείᾳ ("except for unchastity"—Trans.), and παρεκτὸς λόγου

Strecker, *Weg der Gerechtigkeit. Untersuchung zur Theologie des Matthäus* (Göttingen, 1962), pp. 130–2.

πορνείας ("except on the ground of unchastity"—Trans.) in 5. 32 (cf. Acts 26. 29), denote an exception.[17] But there is still a dispute about the state of affairs to which they actually refer.

Two main interpretations are current. The first one treats πορνεία as meaning an *illicit marriage between relatives* (cf. Lev. 18) as it does in Acts 15. 20, 29. So it is not a question of an exceptional case in which the divorce of a valid marriage would be *allowed*, but of the separation *commanded* by the Law of people who were married illegitimately.[18] H. Baltensweiler[19] tried to make this view definitive by reconstructing a community situation in which the interpolation of clauses like this would make sense. He thinks of the Judaeo-Christian communities. Former Jewish proselytes could have contracted illegitimate marriages, for Jewish practice was in their case lax. According to the rules for proselytes, the prohibitions of Leviticus 18 only applied to them in a restricted way. But the Christian community commanded the dissolution of such marriages, which were in their view unlawful (cf. Acts 15. 20). In his "unchastity" clause Matthew excludes these cases from Jesus' prohibition of divorce. So in this view it is not a question of the prohibition being narrowed down, but of the Jewish Law being tightened up; and this is characteristic of Matthew.

According to the second interpretation, the clause *allows* the dissolution of a *valid* marriage. But views differ as to the precise meaning of the term πορνεία, which is the reason for divorce:[20] ordinary unchastity or adultery?; "unbridled, perhaps perverse

---

[17] Cf. H. Baltensweiler, *op. cit.*, p. 90, note 31; A. Sand, *op. cit.*, p. 121; R. Schnackenburg, *The Moral Teaching of the New Testament* (Freiburg, 1965), c. 103.

[18] Cf. J. Bonsirven, *Le divorce dans le Nouveau Testament* (Paris, 1948). Various exegetes have followed him, e.g., J. B. Bauer, "De coniugali foedere quid edixerit Matthaeus? (Mt. 5. 31s.; 19. 3–9)", in *Verb. Dom.*, 44 (1966), pp. 74–8; R. Pesch, *op. cit.*, p. 212; R. Schnackenburg, *op. cit.*, p. 17; *ibid.*, note 15, for further references.

[19] *Op. cit.*, pp. 91–102: "It all depends on whether we can think of an historical situation which would fit the interpretation we have just been developing."

[20] There is a survey of the interpretations in A. Sand, *op. cit.*, p. 125; H. Baltensweiler, *op. cit.*, p. 88 f.; F. Hauck, S. Schulz, *Theol. Dict. of the N.T.*, VI, p. 583, pp. 587–94.

sensuality";[21] a pre-marital lapse on the part of the wife which has only come to light after marriage;[22] or prostitution?[23]

We cannot decide the issue on philological grounds alone, for the word πορνεία is used in many different ways. So we must turn to the second norm of exegesis, the *context*. Now it is quite clear that Matthew 19. 3–9 is dealing with ordinary divorce, not with the subsequent dissolution of illicit marriages. And our examination of Matthew's redaction allows us to go further and draw more exact conclusions. When Matthew changed the basic question in Mark to the question about divorce being allowed for any cause, he revealed a conscious modification of the problem. And the alteration of the reply in v. 9 corresponds to this altered question. Matthew does indeed remain bound to the received tradition, but he adds this clause to Jesus' saying in recognition of the special problems he and his community have to face. Referring to the tradition, he rejects the divorce of one's wife "for any cause", but in his additional clause he does admit an exception to the general prohibition. A key-point for grasping the intellectual background to the problem is given by the formulation of the question and by the clauses themselves (especially that of 5. 32). They refer to the discussion between the school of Schammai and that of Hillel about the grounds for divorce.[24] The clauses have a precise meaning which is derived from their Rabbinic parallels:[25] if his wife is unfaithful, her husband may

---

[21] K. Bornhauser, *The Sermon on the Mount* (Madras, 1935), c. 82.

[22] A. Friedrichsen, "Excepta fornicatione causa", in *Svensk Exegetisk Årsbok*, 9 (1944), pp. 54–8.   [23] A. Sand, *op. cit.*, pp. 127, 128.

[24] The rabbinical discussion is concerned with the interpretation of the expression עֶרְוַת דָּבָר (some indecency) in Deut. 24. 1. The school of Schammai takes the phrase narrowly and only allows divorce when there is really some *indecency* (*unchastity, adultery*). The school of Hillel takes it widely to mean *anything* objectionable: "Even if she has let his food get burnt", it remarks pointedly. Cf. Billerbeck, *op. cit.*, I, p. 313; and F. Hauck, S. Schulz, *Theol. Dict. of the N.T.*, VI, pp. 587 f.; G. Strecker, *op. cit.*, p. 132, note 3, who emphasizes the relevant point that "the important parallel with the adultery clause in the school of Schammai is characteristic not of the evangelist but of the historically rooted circumstances of his community".

[25] πορνεία can be understood in this sense, as is shown by the parallels collected by F. Hauck, S. Schulz, *Theol. Dict. of the N.T.*, VI, pp. 584 f., 587 f.; and by H. T. Wrege, *Die Überlieferungsgeschichte der Bergpredigt* (Tübingen, 1968), p. 68. Cf., e.g., Sir. 23. 23c: ἐν πορνείᾳ ἐμοιχεύθη.

divorce her and marry again.[26] For, as we can in this view infer from the dispute, her unfaithfulness has destroyed the original created unity of the marriage.

An analysis of Matthew 5. 31 f. leads to the same result. Comparison with Luke 16. 18 shows that Matthew took the saying from the Q source and himself placed it in its antithetical framework so that it could take its place among the antitheses of the Sermon on the Mount. For his Old Testament premise he chooses the classic divorce text of Deuteronomy 24. 1, but he omits the condition included in this text: "because he has found some indecency in her". In this way he arrives at a formulation which allows divorce without any limit being set (as also in 19. 3). In opposition to this "commandment" he sets Jesus' reading of the Law. He formulates v. 32a (which diverges from Lk. 16. 18a) in accordance with Deuteronomy 24. 1 and with Jewish practice, both of which presume remarriage on the part of the wife. And he does this in such a way that the remarriage is taken into account and charged up to the husband as an offence: he "makes her an adulteress". But if she has already committed adultery he is not guilty, for she has herself broken the marriage by her deed.

In both these places it seems from the context highly unlikely that Matthew's clauses were referring to illegitimate marriages. On the contrary, his redaction confirms the second view, which sees the clauses as admitting in the case of adultery an exception to the commandment on divorce.

But is this interpretation compatible with the way Matthew expounds the Law—he generally seems to intensify its demands? And in fact such intensification is certainly present in the call for greater righteousness (Mt. 5. 20) which is the main theme of his exposition of the Law in the Sermon on the Mount. Matthew's intentions, however, do not end there. He is also concerned to make Jesus' demands feasible.[27] It is for this reason that he

---

[26] Cf. above all the more recent investigations into the redaction-history of Matthew: G. Bornkamm in G. Bornkamm, G. Barth, H. J. Held, *Tradition and Interpretation in Matthew* (Philadelphia, 1963), c. 23; G. Barth, *ibid.*, c. 89; G. Strecker, *op. cit.*, p. 132; R. Hummel, *op. cit.*, p. 51; H. T. Wrege, *op. cit.*, p. 69.

[27] Cf. Strecker, *op. cit.*, p. 132.

explains the prohibition of anger (5. 22a) by means of the prohibition of insults (5. 22b, c); and he turns the absolute prohibition of swearing oaths into a recommendation of the formula "Yes, yes"—"No, no" through which God's name will not be misused.[28] So Matthew does not merely heighten the Law's demands in a radical way; he is also prepared to modify them. But his modifications still surpass the "righteousness of the scribes and Pharisees", as is clear from a comparison with the common practice sanctioned by these groups. His interpretation of the saying on divorce fits in perfectly with this basic attitude of his.

3. *1 Corinthians 7. 10 f., 12–16*

In 1 Corinthians 7 Paul is dealing with particular questions put by the Christians of Corinth (7. 1). It was evidently, from ascetical motives, considered the ideal there to keep away from marriage and sexual intercourse altogether. And in his reply Paul also shows a preference for the unmarried state. This is primarily because he expects the Second Coming of the Lord in the immediate future. But for him celibacy is not a law, it is a charism —a free gift of God, only binding those to whom it is given (7. 7). So he approves of marriage too, and recommends it to those who, by reason of their very vitality, see it to be their way.

The remarks on divorce occur in this context.[29] In 1 Corinthians 7. 10 f. Paul turns his attention to married people and refers to the Lord's commandment; but he does not quote it literally—"To the married I give charge, not I but the Lord, that the wife should not separate from her husband . . . and that the husband should not divorce his wife". Like Mark (10. 11 f.), Paul presupposes a tradition in which Jesus' words have been adapted to the conditions of life under Hellenic-Roman law. He formulates the commandment in a fundamental way which corresponds with that of Mark 10. 9; there too the separation of the

---

[28] Cf. P. Hoffmann, *op. cit.*, pp. 181–6.

[29] For what follows cf. above all H. Conzelmann, *op. cit.*, pp. 143 f. (refs. to lit.); H. Baltensweiler, *op. cit.*, pp. 187–96; H. von Campenhausen, "Die Begründung kirchlicher Entscheidung beim Apostel Paulus", in *Aus der Frühzeit des Christentums* (Tübingen, 1963), pp. 52 f.; W. Schrage, *Die konkreten Einzelgebote in der paulinischen Paränese* (Gütersloh, 1961), pp. 241–3; O. Merk, *Handeln aus Glauben. Die Motivierung der paulinischen Ethik* (Marburg, 1968), pp. 104–15.

partners is forbidden absolutely. But for Paul this "commandment" of the Lord is not a rigid rule. He adds to it the gloss:
"but if she does separate (or has separated),[30] let her remain single
or else be reconciled with her husband" (v. 11a). He may here be
admitting a general exception or, as is more likely, be concerned
only with one particular case in which the wife has already left
her husband. But at all events he does modify the absoluteness of
the commandment when he turns his attention to the particular
situation of an individual.

In 7. 12–16 Paul, on his own authority, takes up a stand with
regard to marriages between a pagan and a Christian. The special
problems these marriages present to the community force him to
find a ruling which stems from the "commandment" of the Lord
but goes beyond it. The way he does this is "instructive for the
relationship between law and freedom".[31] The first question is
whether such marriages should be allowed to continue in existence at all (v. 11, 14). And then, when in v. 14 he so forcibly
emphasizes the fact that the unbelieving partner will be "consecrated" by the believer, his words reveal the existence in Corinth
of a particular prejudice: fear of being made unholy by intercourse with one's pagan marriage-partner.[32] Paul argues against
this, reasoning that Christ has brought us freedom. The Christian
party to such a marriage does not fall prey to the "evil world-
powers"; rather, he consecrates his pagan partner, bringing
her into the dimension of God's love. It is possible to live together without fear. The Christian does not have to separate on
religious grounds; indeed on those very grounds he must not.

The decision of his unbelieving partner is the determining
factor for the Christian. If the pagan party wants to continue life
together, the Christian should not choose divorce. "But if the unbelieving partner desires to separate, let it be so." And he continues, "in such a case the brother or sister is not bound" (v. 15).
Paul accepts the decision made by the pagan as changing the
married status of the Christian, and includes this as a factor in

---

[30] The aorist subjunctive allows of both translations.
[31] H. Conzelmann, *op. cit.*, p. 145.
[32] Cf. above all J. Blinzler, "Zur Auslegung von 1 Kor. 7, 14", in *Neutestamentliche Aufsätze*, Festschrift für J. Schmid (Munich, 1963), pp. 32–
41; and H. Conzelmann, *op. cit.*, pp. 146–8.

his exposition of the "commandment". And he draws the conclusion that the Christian too is in this case free from his obligation to his partner (and to the "commandment"). There is no express mention of remarriage. That is understandable in view of the attitude taken by the Corinthians to marriage, and of Paul's expectation of the Second Coming. But the principle of the revocation of marital obligations is so strongly formulated that the Christian partner may well in fact be free to enter a second marriage if he wants to.[33]

In 7. 15c Paul adds a reference to the peace to which God has called us.[34] Peace—*shalom*—is an idea full of meaning. It is rooted in the traditional greeting of the Jewish people. In Paul's usage it extends to final eschatological salvation, but also to that peace which God can bestow on human life-together. Following here on 7. 15b it may well be referring (as it does in 1 Cor. 14. 33) to freedom from quarrelling and strife, to well-being and happiness —without, of course, losing its theological dimension on this account.

In 7. 16–24 Paul adds some reflections which reveal the process behind his argumentation: every man should change his state only so far as God has called him to do so, and the Lord given him the gift. A man's talents, his position in life, his historical situation are all determined individually. These are his limits, and within these limits God gives the possibility of salvation, freedom, love and new existence. God in his saving work accepts these premises, so the Christian must accept them too. This means, with reference to the way he argues in the matter of

[33] A comparison with the form of expression in 7. 39 (cf. Rom. 7. 2 f.) strongly suggests that οὐ δεδούλωται be read in this radical manner: there δένεται is used for the bond of the woman to her husband, ἐλευθέρα for her freedom.

[34] The sense of v. 16 is disputed. J. Jeremias, "Die missionarische Aufgabe in der Mischehe", in *Neutestamentliche Studien für R. Bultmann* (Berlin, ²1957), pp. 225–60, sees v. 16 as referring to the possible conversion of the pagan husband: "How do you know that you will not save your husband?" In that case "peace" in v. 15b would mean reconciliation with the husband. But the context as a whole points to the fact that εἰ (v. 16) be read as "whether" rather than as εἰ μή ("that ... not"): "How do you know whether you will save your husband?" Verse 16 guards against too much missionary zeal. Cf. H. Conzelmann, *op. cit.*, p. 149, note 48.

divorce, that Paul too accepts the realities of the situation in which the Christian finds himself through his partner's decision, and which he cannot alter. And in this situation Paul accords him the right to freedom and peace.

III. SUMMARY AND CONCLUSION

In his teaching on divorce Jesus does *not* lay down a *law*, but rather reveals the *reality* of marriage, and does so precisely in opposition to any legal narrowing of the issues. "Jesus reaches behind the plane of the Law to that of the Law's origins, so his words must not in their turn be taken directly and simply as law."[35] The *demands* made by marriage do of course become apparent when its reality is laid bare—it is certainly true that Jesus' words are moral directives.

Jesus made manifest the irrevocable unity of marriage. We can suppose that the Marcan community wanted to ground this unity in an appeal to Genesis 1, 2, by going right back to God's creative act. The theological postulate "What God has put together let not man put asunder" follows clearly from that. "Separation" too, not just divorce and remarriage, disrupts God's original order.

But if this strong demand of marriage was to take effect in the community it would have to undergo in the course of the Christian tradition a process of application to concrete instances. The Christian groups growing up at this time needed clear commandments. The New Testament shows that this process came about in many different ways. Jesus' demand was conceived as an ethical directive (cf. Lk. 16. 18 in its context), or even as a legal ruling (cf. Mt. 19. 9 and 5. 32 in the light of Mt. 28. 19).

But what factors determine these changes? Some variations are due to a particular cultural background: Jesus' saying with the demands it made had to be explained in one way for Jews and in another for Greeks, if it was to be understood at all (cf. Mk. 10. 12; 1 Cor. 7. 10 f. as opposed to the re-judaizing of Mt. 19 and 5. 31 f.).

There is, however, a second and more decisive factor. The process of expounding Jesus' saying brought modifications which

[35] J. Ratzinger, *op. cit.*, p. 83.

seem to weaken that saying's radical demands. But this is clearly a necessary step—the step of taking account of human faults in marriage. And, being such, it shows that the Christian community, while avowing its dependence on and subjection to Jesus' word, did not think of this word as law but as an imperative which for ever calls out for new interpretation.

This process began immediately Jesus' words, which first presented rather a pictorial impression, began to be read in a literal sense, with the consequent deduction that divorce and remarriage were forbidden (Mk. 10. 11 and possibly Q and Lk. 16. 18 too. Paul gives this concession in his own gloss 1 Cor. 7. 11a). This reading does indeed give the impression that theoretically the "indissolubility" of marriage is not in question, but *de facto* here too the marriage has already been suspended. A theologically more explosive question is the problem raised by Matthew's adultery clause and by Paul's dissolution of pagan-Christian marriages.

Matthew allows divorce in the case of adultery by the one partner (it is because of his Jewish background that he speaks only of unfaithfulness by the woman). But on the other hand he critically confronts the Jewish divorce "for any cause" with the irrevocable unity of marriage rooted in Genesis 1, 2. He evidently knows cases where the unity of marriage can be so destroyed by the unfaithfulness of one partner that it *de facto* ceases to exist, with the result that remarriage is possible. It is true that rabbinical discussion may not have been without its influence on him here, but there is no doubt at all of the fact that he intends this solution of his to be understood as a commandment of the Lord. The irrevocable unity of marriage stands in Matthew as a *theological postulate* in tension with that unity which men have to realize *in their own history*, and often enough cannot realize properly.

Paul is confronted with what was a new question for Christians of his day: how should they judge the divorce of pagan-Christian marriages? He makes it quite clear that the Christian is bound to keep the Lord's "commandment" if the pagan party does not want divorce. But if his partner does want it, the Christian is released from his obligation. Paul accepts the historical situation in which the Christian is put by the decision of his partner. This is for him not just a concession; it presupposes a theological understanding of the individual situation. God in his saving work accepts this situation; his gift of freedom, his call to peace, are addressed to the Christian precisely in this situation. So these individual factors must also be taken into account when it comes to expounding the "commandment" of the Lord. One can interpret the reference to freedom (1 Cor. 7. 15) in different ways, but in my opinion it shows too that in this conflict between "commandment" and "concrete situation" we must not overlook the fact that man is called to peace and happiness. So in principle both of these factors must be given proper weight in any interpretation: the demand for irrevocable unity in marriage, *and* the situation in which man finds himself.

This essay calls for development of the discussion not only in the field of theology but in that of canon law as well, so that we too in our present-day Church practice may do justice to the demand made by Jesus and to its interpretation in the New Testament.

Translated by J. T. Swann

Korbinian Ritzer

Secular Law and the Western Church's Concept of Marriage

I. The Common Ground between all Divine and Human Law

WITHIN the sphere of the Roman imperium it was to the advantage of the teaching of Christ and of his Church that Roman marriage was monogamous in origin and tradition. A permanent marriage bond among the Romans excluded on principle any other marriage, or any relationship similar to marriage, such as concubinage.[1] This was certainly in keeping with the basic marriage customs of the Indo-Germanic races, but was also, it is clear, typically Roman. It is, however, true that the definition of marriage as "an entire partnership in life, which embraces both divine and human law", formulated in these words by Herennius Modestinus, one of the last of Rome's classical jurists (3rd century A.D.), already finds an echo with the Greeks.[2] But it was clearly in complete accord with Roman sentiment. In the so-called manus-marriage, which would seem to have been the rule in the

[1] Cf. M. Kaser, *Röm. Privatrecht*, I (Munich, 1955), pp. 67–74, 260, 190; II (1959), pp. 107, 141; Pauly-Wissowa-Kroll, *Realenc. d. class. Altertumswiss*, esp. the arts. "matrimonium" (Kunkel: 14 [1930], pp. 2259 ff.), "nuptiae" (Ehrhardt: 17 [1936], pp. 1478 ff.); K. Ritzer, *Formen, Riten u. religiöses Brauchtum d. Eheschliessung in den christl. Kirchen d. erst. Jahrtausends* (Münster, 1962); A. Oepke, *Eke: Reallex. f. Antike u. Christent.*, IV (1959), pp. 650, 666; *ibid.*, further articles on "Ehebruch", "gesetze", etc.

[2] "Consortium omnis vitae, divini et humani iuris communicatio" (*Dig.* 23, 2, 1 Modestin); further evidence in Ehrhardt, *loc. cit.*, 1482; also E. von Lasaulx, "Zur Gesch. u. Philosophie d. Ehe bei den Griechen", in *Abhandl. d. Bay. Akad. d. Wissensch. Philos.-Philol. Kl.*, 7, 1 (Munich, 1853), pp. 33 f., note 22.

republican days of Rome, the woman lost her former family status, and from now onwards came under the protective power (*manus, patria potestas*) of her husband. It was her duty to serve him and his tribe as *mater familias*, and present him with children, but also to take part in the family cultus of the family or tribe into which she had been received. The continuance of the line, and especially the production of male heirs, served among other purposes to foster the cult of the family, which could, if there was any danger of its dying out, be guaranteed survival, if need be, by adoption from other families. This religio-cultic sensitivity was responsible for the development of very fully evolved wedding customs at the very beginning of marriage; and the solemnity was maintained in houses of some social standing even when in the so-called free marriage the wife continued to belong to her previous family circle and was no longer subject to her husband's protective power. The solemn wedding ritual bound up with the "handing-over" of the woman in the *confarreatio*, which was always reserved for the old patrician families and was obligatory for certain priestly offices, was even instrumental in maintaining and furthering the worship of the State.

In early Christian times the ideals often corresponded very little with reality. Augustus failed in his marriage law reforms, by which he hoped to check the moral decline in order to keep the leading families in being and strengthen Italy's military potential. Yet the thought embodied in the Modestinus precept could still serve early Christianity as a point of departure for the development of its new ideal of marriage from the spirit of revelation and the wisdom of philosophy. Did the early Christians make full enough use of these possibilities? No doubt we are far from well informed about the full content of early Christian preaching, and about early Christian family life and its effectiveness as a witness to the Gospel. The fact that the young Church held fast to the validity of the Old Testament, and so to marriage as a divine ordinance, gave it the strongest of weapons against the Gnostic doctrines and other tendencies hostile to marriage.[3]

[3] Cf. K. Ritzer, "Ehe in der alten Kirche", in *Werk-material z. Brautleutekurs*, 5 (printed in manuscript Verl. Haus Altenberg, Düsseldorf, 1966), p. 4.

In Book II of his *Ad Uxorem* (written to his wife), Tertullian vividly describes the burdens that had to be put up with by a Christian woman married to a pagan; and he praises the marriage in which the Church brings both partners together, and encourages the regular reception of the Eucharist in community worship and in house services.[4] Unfortunately, Tertullian subsequently lessened the value of his comments by his unseemly judgment upon a second marriage entered into by a Christian husband after the death of his first partner. "Insidious dualism and montanistic rigorism make a strange alliance", says Albrecht Oepke. Not only is there a prejudice with regard to a new marriage after the first partner's death, which—according to the Pastoral Epistles—excluded a man from priestly office, and called forth from the apologist Athenagoras the description of a second marriage as "respectable adultery",[5] but the attitude of the Church's writings in general towards marriage is characterized by disapproval of the sexual element, in so far as it was not directly linked to procreation.

The interpretation which confined the divine paradisal blessing to the first marriage only led to the prohibition in the Roman liturgy against allowing the solemn marriage blessing, bound up as it was with the wedding Mass, to be used for bigamists. In this connection Pope Innocent I (401–417) stressed the ruling that anyone must also be reckoned a bigamist who had already been married as a pagan and then contracted a second marriage as a Christian. "For baptism does indeed wash away sins, but not a number of wives."[6] In the same way, a bridal pair lost their claim to a liturgical blessing if even one of the partners had committed sins of unchastity before marriage. And so for hundreds of years, wherever the Roman liturgy prevailed—which was soon almost the whole of the Western world—such pairs were excluded from any liturgical solemnization of the beginnings of their marriage, and in this way were limited to secular marriage forms and customs, and forced into the position of penitents.

[4] For this passage (II, 8), cf. Ritzer, *Formen*, pp. 58–67.

[5] *Legatio*, 33 (p. 152, ed. Geffcken); in connection with the rite of blessing for marriage, cf. Ritzer, *Formen*, p. 57, and *passim*; B. Kötting, *Digamus*, III (1957), pp. 1016, 1024.

[6] A letter to Archbishop Victricius of Rouen; cf. Ritzer, *Formen*, pp. 164 and 168, note 69.

We shall have to agree with Oepke in his thoroughly positive judgment of the religious values and sources of strength which Christianity opened up to married people, combined, however, with the assertion that "the spiritual idea of marriage was worked out in philosophy quite independently of Christianity. Measured by this standard, Christianity of the first few centuries was by no means 'modern' or 'progressive', but rather 'conservative', if not 'reactionary'."

II. SUB LEGE CUSTODIEBAMUR INCLUSI (GAL. 3. 24)

A painful chapter in the Church's history, as far as the law of marriage is concerned, is constituted by the impediments to marriage, especially as they existed up to the Fourth Lateran Council (1215).[7] Linking up her practice with the Old Testament, particularly Leviticus 18 and 20, as well as with the law and customs of Rome, the Western Church placed a series of impediments against marriage between blood-relations and between those already related by marriage. The Book of Leviticus forbids marriage between a man and his mother or sisters, and with the sisters of his parents, as well as with the daughters of his sons and daughters. Roman law and custom forbade all marriage links in the direct line between brothers and sisters, but also with uncles and aunts, great-uncles and great-aunts. In the year 384 the Emperor Theodosius I also forbade marriage between the children of brothers and sisters. And the jurist Paullus (about A.D. 200) is even said to have pronounced as impermissible marriage between great-grandchildren and great-nieces (*Dig.* 23, 2, 39 pr.). In accordance with the principles of Roman reckoning, "as many degrees as there were procreations", this amounts to the fifth degree. By this reckoning, brothers and sisters were related in the first degree, brothers and sisters' children in the second, since the acts of procreation were only taken into account on one side until you reached back to a common ancestor.

The Church reformers who concealed themselves behind the pseudo-Isidorian forgeries, and flourished about the middle of the

---

[7] Cf. A. Esmein and E. Génestal, *Le mariage en droit canonique*, I (Paris, 1929), pp. 227 ff.; G. H. Joyce, *Die christl. Ehe* (Leipzig, 1934), pp. 447 ff.

ninth century, did in fact extend the impediments to matrimony, prohibiting it and invalidating it to such an extreme that it even reached the seventh degree. The impediments arising from relationship by marriage, from pre-marital or extra-marital relationships with blood-relations on the other side and from incest, all of which prevented the accomplishment of a valid marriage or the continuance of an already accomplished and consummated union—these also grew in very much the same proportions. It was to one of these last impediments that a certain Count Stephen of Aquitaine appealed, in the days of Hincmar, archbishop of Rheims. The Count maintained that his marriage was invalid because, previous to this union, he had had illicit intercourse with a relation of his wife's. In the eleventh century Roman synods began to use all their influence for this extensive range of matrimonial impediments. To be sure, an enlightened canonical scholarship did subsequently demolish these over-extensive impediments to marriage, and showed that not all these precepts—even if contained in the Old Testament—were unalterable and divinely appointed ordinances, and that the Pope possessed extensive powers to make dispensations from the strictly legal line. The Fourth Lateran Council reduced the impediments to marriage (Canon 21, X, IV 14, 8) to a viable level.

Every secular and every ecclesiastical law is exposed to the danger of misuse through attempts to make the weaker cause appear the stronger. When the Emperor Lothair II (855–869) wanted to discard his wedded wife Teutberga, he accused her of pre-marital incest.[8] In the time of Innocent III, King Philip Augustus of France wanted to achieve the dissolution of his union with a Danish princess on the grounds of impediments to marriage which were sought for and discovered subsequently to the event.[9] In England, Henry VIII married with papal dispensation his brother's widow, Catherine of Aragon, and subsequently disputed the papal right to give this dispensation in order to clear the way for his desired union with Anne Boleyn.[10] Law and conscience, justice and the pure teaching of the gospels, will always remain in mutual tension. When the Melchite Patriarchal Vicar

[8] Cf. Joyce, loc. cit., pp. 314, 316.   [9] Cf. ibid., pp. 343 f.
[10] Cf. ibid., pp. 477, 479.

of Egypt, Elias Zoghbi, intervened in the Second Vatican Council debate on 29 September 1965 in order to defend the Eastern Church's practice, based upon the "Matthean exception" for adultery (Matt. 19. 9), of allowing an innocent divorced partner to contract a second marriage, he considered he had justifiable grounds for criticizing the practice of matrimonial courts in the West. He maintained that a casuistic subtlety often exercised almost acrobatic ingenuity in its efforts to discover, even after ten or twenty years of marriage, some impediment that would be able, like a magic wand, to declare the union null and void.[11]

III. LIBERORUM QUAERENDORUM CAUSA

To the Israelites of the Old Testament, plenty of children were a sign of God's blessing. Clement of Alexandria says that marriage is a duty to the succeeding generations, to one's fatherland, and to the replenishment of the world.[11a] The Roman Censors, whose office had indeed fallen into disuse since Sulla's reforms, required of a citizen who was capable of marriage an oath that he would take a wife in order to raise up lawful seed. In the year 231 B.C. a Roman citizen, appealing to this oath, deserted his wife when she continued to be barren—the first historically attested divorce in Rome. As Augustine of Hippo testifies, the written marriage contracts that had become very common since the early Empire set forth the purpose of marriage as the procreation of descendants.[12] In his work entitled *De bono coniugali*, Augustine links the trinity of blessings "offspring, faithfulness and sacrament" (*proles, fides, sacramentum*) asyndetically with one another.[13] These threefold values, especially the *"sacramentum"* that is so closely linked with indissolubility, prompted early Scholasticism to give marriage a place among the seven sacraments. This crops up again in the Florentine Decree of Union for the Armenians,[14] as well as in the encyclical *Casti connubi* of Pius XI (1931).[15] Mention should also be made here of the setting forth,

---

[11] "Deutscher Auszug aus d. Interv. v. 22.9.1965", in J. Chr. Hampe, *Autorität der Freiheit*, III (Munich, 1967), p. 266.
[11a] *Strom.*, II, 23, 140, 1; cf. Lasaulx, *loc. cit.*, p. 27, note 9.
[12] Ritzer, *Formen*, pp. 27 f. (note 138 f.).   [13] PL 40, 394.
[14] Denzinger-Schönmetzer, *Enchr. Symbolor*, n. 1327 (702).
[15] *Ibid.*, n. 3703 (2227 ff.).

in Canon 1013 of the *Codex Iuris Canonici*, of the procreation and upbringing of children as the chief purpose of marriage.

The Fathers of the Second Vatican Council did not find it easy to wrestle with the problems of achieving a new vision of what "the good things of marriage" really are. One might point to Cardinal Suenens' anxious question, "whether we have not too much underlined the first aim of marriage—the continuation of the race—to the detriment of an equally requisite aim of marriage—the growth of conjugal unity";[16] and likewise to the words of the Pastoral Constitution *Gaudium et Spes* (49) on the moral dignity of those acts which, when accomplished in a spirit of human respect, enable man and wife to express their "mutual committal, and thus enrich their sense of joy and gratitude".

IV. Nuptias non concubitus, sed consensus facit

The historians of Roman Law tell us that Roman marriage was not in the first place a legal relationship, but a social condition or state.[17] It depended on the matrimonial disposition (*affectio maritalis*) expressing itself in the corresponding behaviour of the partners, and was to be measured not by juridical, but by social standards. For the duration of the marriage, which according to classical law was terminable at any time by either partner, the woman occupied the position of wedded wife. If she was free-born, it was presumed that she was acting out of matrimonial intention. It is true that the bridal pair, who were still under the authority of a *pater familias*, were dependent upon his approval both for the betrothal and for the marriage. But the paternal power was to be used benevolently, and the prospective partners were expected to give their free and unforced consent.

The Christian emperors took extensive account of Christian principles in their legislation. They either could not or would not entirely abolish the right to separation in marriage. In general, too, they held fast to the principle of the formal freedom of the marriage relationship. In 542, the Emperor Justinian made it obligatory only for persons of senatorial rank to draw up written marriage contracts. He rescinded the requirements of 538 that

[16] *Interv. v. 30.10.1964*; cf. Hampe, *loc. cit.*, p. 259.
[17] Cf. Kaser, 1, 65.

persons of the middle class must provide themselves with a written marriage testimonial signed by an official of the Church (*defensor ecclesiae*) and three or four clergy. Even the Popes, whose word—since the extinction of the Western Empire—became of increasing weight, gave their support in general to the formal freedom of matrimony. In clear and sharp contrast to the Greek developments, in 866 Pope Nicholas I informed the Bulgars, who had only recently become Christians, that the contract of marriage did not depend either on secular custom, or on ecclesiastical rites, but exclusively upon the intention to marry which the law required of the prospective partners.[18] Without this, the Pope emphasized, even sexual intercourse did not constitute a legal marriage. The one and only essential for marriage —an intention to marry by the partners—was no less strongly emphasized by his successor, Hadrian II (867–872).[19] These papal pronouncements were all the more important because from about the end of the tenth century the Church courts had enjoyed almost exclusive and undisputed jurisdiction over all matrimonial cases. This situation arose partly from the fact that in an age of great legal fragmentation in the West, the Church alone was in a position to lay down universally valid standards.

The Canonist and Scholastic learning that came in with the eleventh century took up the lead given by Roman Law, which was then undergoing a kind of renaissance, and by Pope Nicholas I.[20] Since the time of Ivo of Chartres (d. 1117), it insisted with increasing sharpness upon the distinction between an intention to marry directed to the present, and one directed to the future, on the part of the prospective partners. In the former (*consensus de praesenti*) one can clearly discern the motive that lies at the basis of marriage. In the teaching of Peter Lombard (d. 1160) "the *Sponsaliendistinktion* became the foundation of a completely self-contained scholastic doctrinal system".[21] And this does not

[18] Cf. Ritzer, *Formen*, pp. 340 f. and *passim*.

[19] PL 122, 1318.

[20] Cf. H. Portmann, *Wesen u. Unauflöslichk. d. Ehe, Ehe in d. Kirchl. Wissenschaft u. Gesetzgeb. d. 11. u. 12. Jahrh. Ein Beitrag z. kirchl. Rechtsgesch* (Emsdetten-Westf., 1938), esp. pp. 37–70; Joyce, *loc. cit.*, p. 177; for the liturgical connection with the development of *ordines ad facienda sponsalia*, see also Ritzer, *Formen*, pp. 295–306, 313.

[21] Portman, *loc. cit.*, pp. 42 f.

only apply to the legal aspect. Peter Lombard was the first theologian to fix the seven sacraments. He stresses in his *Sentences* that it is exclusively the "consent"—the willing assent of both partners—that constitutes marriage (IV, 24, 2; PL 192, 915). He disputes the verdict of the pseudo-Isidorian false decretals of Pope Evaristus (about the year 100). All that the reformers of the ninth century had stressed as particularly important—the orderly conclusion of the marriage contract, the wooing of the bride by the relatives, the betrothal, the dowry, the priestly blessing and the public wedding—all this is brushed aside as meaningless. He admits that it serves to increase the outward show and respectability of the marriage, but it is not essential for the validity of the sacramental marriage bond. Only the secretly given consent, he holds, constitutes a sacramental marriage, even if secret matrimony remained unlawful. This means for one thing that the sacramental bond of marriage is only accomplished through the recognizably expressed and willed decision of the prospective couple. It might almost be said, then, that husband and wife administer the sacrament to themselves and to their partner.

But there was another difficulty too, which even Peter Lombard recognized. The Church courts remained up to the Council of Trent with an often insoluble task, for the contraction of clandestine marriages could mostly not be proved. Other questions, such as the possibilities for dissolving a marriage before it has been consummated by sexual union, as well as the importance of this for the ultimate indissolubility of marriage, proved less difficult of solution.

Translated by J. E. Anderson

Nicolaas van der Wal

Secular Law and the Eastern Church's Concept of Marriage

I. DIVORCE

IN classical Roman law[1] marriage was a factual situation which persisted because—and as long as—both partners wanted to live in the married state. At some point, difficult to determine but definitely before A.D. 600, this concept changed under the influence of Christianity: marriage came about by contractual agreement between the partners and persisted also if the partners no longer wanted to live together. The classical concept naturally implied that both partners remained completely free to opt for a divorce, even unilaterally.

After the introduction of Christianity, divorce was tied to various explicit reasons, though these reasons varied in number and nature. A divorce without such a valid reason was punished with grave penalties affecting the partner's worldly fortune, but the divorce was granted.

The Emperor Justinian (529–65) tightened up this legislation to the point of condemning the guilty partner to join a religious order. This same sanction applied also to divorce by mutual agreement so that guilty divorcees could not remarry.

[1] General literature: K. E. Zachariä von Lingenthal, *Geschichte des griechischrömischen Rechts* (Aalen, 1955), pp. 55–83; J. Dauvillier and C. de Clerq, *Le mariage en droit canonique oriental* (Paris, 1936); O. Rousseau, "Divorce and Remarriage: East and West", in *Concilium* (April 1967), pp. 57–69 (American edn., vol. 24, pp. 113–38). See also N. van der Wal, *Manuale Novellarum Justiniani* (Groningen, 1964), pp. 64–71.

Curiously enough, the same Justinian who, in the 22nd *Novella* still quoted Plato to prove that any contract between human beings can be dissolved,[2] decreed a few years later that divorce without valid reasons was not only forbidden, but also null and void.[3] But this nullity, already ignored by contemporary commentators, disappeared from later legal practice without leaving any trace.

Not until the eighth century did the *Ecloga*, the legal code of the iconoclastic emperors, link the law of marriage and divorce with Matthew 5. 32 and 19. 9, and then the quotation is followed by a number of reasons for divorce.[4] The cases enumerated there are fewer than in Justinian's legislation, but several of them (attempted murder of the partner and the husband's impotence, for instance) cannot possibly be tied up with the fornication (*pornéia*) of the gospel text, and a new one, leprosy, is added for the first time.

After the restoration of Orthodoxy the various codifications went back to the system of Justinian, and legal practice became even more supple than the theory. This is clear from the *Pira Eustathii Romani*, a collection of reports of cases judged by Eustathius at the beginning of the eleventh century. Here we meet, for instance, a case of divorce by mutual agreement in writing[5] where both parties granted each other the right to enter upon a second marriage. When, years after, the man died, there was a case about the financial clauses contained in the divorce contract. The judge did not even mention the rule that this divorce should have been punished with the confinement of both parties in a monastery but simply established that, since the woman did not use her right to remarry, the marriage must be deemed to have continued till the man's death.

This also shows that the classical Roman view, according to which a marriage rests on the continuing will to remain married, was completely forgotten in the tenth century.

This case may also provide us with at least one possible

[2] *Nov. Just.*, 22, c. 3: *to hoehen hapan luton*.
[3] *Nov. Just.*, 134, c. 11.
[4] *Ecl.* 2, 12–13 (*Ius Graeco-Romanum*, cura J. et P. Zepi, vol. II, Athens, 1931, pp. 25–6).
[5] *Pira*, 25, 62 (*Ius Graeco-Rom.*, vol. IV, pp. 107–9).

explanation of the difference, so baffling at first sight, between the Roman Catholic and Greek Orthodox views of divorce. For we see here that, in their interpretation of Matthew 19. 9, they were less concerned with divorce itself, but rather with the possible second marriage, an interpretation encouraged somewhat by the formulation of this text.

A more important point, however, is that the Roman Catholic teaching on the seven sacraments was only fully elaborated in the Middle Ages. St Augustine's teaching on this point was still rather ragged and lacked the precision of later formulations.

To this should be added that the Latin Fathers were never very well known in the Greek East, and that, when cultural contact between East and West became scarce after the sixth century, they were no longer read at all.

When the Greeks think of a "sacrament" they think first of all of such things as baptism and ordination. Moreover, however much one can justify the Vulgate's translation of *musterion* by *sacramentum*, it is easy to see that when the Greeks read Paul's description of marriage as a great mystery (*musterion*), this would evoke other associations than when Western European theologians read this text in the light of the teaching of the sacraments as they have been taught it in the Western tradition.

Then there is still, of course, Matthew 19. 6 ("Man must not divide what God has united"), which is much more frequently quoted in Byzantine canon law than Ephesians 5. 32. But this text follows Matthew 19. 9 ("I am not speaking of fornication") too closely for these two texts not to be interpreted together.

The Byzantine interpretation of *porneia* (fornication) in Matthew 19. 9 is interesting for two reasons. First of all, their secular law shows that this word was given a very broad meaning. It was understood as one of various possible reasons for divorce; it not only covered misbehaviour on the part of the woman, but was taken to refer also to that of the man, and—still more strikingly —it was also taken to cover reasons which could not possibly imply guilt on the part of either partner, such as impotence and leprosy.

Secondly, it is even more interesting for us today to see how Basil the Great, the foremost authority in this matter, interpreted this text of Matthew.[6] Basil links Matthew 19. 9 with two texts from the Old Testament, Jeremiah 3. 1 and Proverbs 18. 22a ("The man who keeps an adulterous wife is foolish and impious",[7] a text which exists in the Septuagint but is lacking in most current versions of the Hebrew Old Testament), and he concludes that a man not only may but *must* divorce his adulterous wife.

The Council of Neocaesarea[8] also imposed this obligation on those of the lower clergy who had an adulterous wife. All this shows how behaviour which juridically created the possibility of divorce became a duty to divorce in early Byzantine moral theology,[9] although only in the case mentioned in Matthew 19. 9, understood literally.

All this explains how the Byzantines came to consider divorce as possible in principle, but not yet how they came to accept, apparently without difficulty, the extension of this possibility to circumstances which had no connection whatever with the fornication of Matthew 19. 9.

One of the circumstances which contributed to this state of affairs was, no doubt, the fact that, in contrast to Western practice, matters of marriage and divorce were not assigned to a separate ecclesiastical tribunal. Particularly at the beginning of the early Byzantine period, when a large number of the empire's citizens were still pagan, it was only natural to leave these matters to the secular authority and to limit Church intervention to the imposition of ecclesiastical penance in extreme cases.

One cannot help wondering, though, why the clergy seem to have made no attempt at having the law changed so that divorce would be allowed only in the case of an adulterous wife (and, for instance, when one of the partners entered a monastery). In the

---

[6] Quoted from *Ioannis Scholastici Synagoga L titulorum*, ed. by V. Beneševič (Munich, 1937), p. 131 (tit. 42, c. 4). I did not have time to look up the original text of Basil's letter.

[7] *Ho de katechon moichalida aphron kai asebes.*

[8] *Synagoga L titulorum*, tit. 41, c. 3 (p. 128 in the above-quoted edition).

[9] In the art. quoted in note 1 Rousseau suggests that Basil places this repudiation of the adulterous wife in secular law, a fact which he tolerates without approval or disapproval. Such an obligation did indeed exist in classical Roman law, but it is doubtful whether this was still felt as valid in Cappadocia in Basil's time. It seems more probable to me that Basil based himself directly on Prov. 18. 22a.

earlier days it may be that the old concept of marriage as resting
on the factual situation created by the continuing agreement of
both partners to remain married still lingered on in people's
minds. This might explain that divorce was indeed forbidden
but could not be declared null and void. Even then, it would
have been possible to forbid remarriage after divorce. But this
kind of argument loses its force for the later period.

In the later period the Greek Orthodox claimed the right to
attenuate over-severe biblical precepts since a stringent application of such precepts would lead to grave frictions in the imperfect society in which man has to live. This flexible dispensation (*oikonomia*) could explain for a large part why the divorce
laws are less rigid in the Byzantine Church.

This position may have been reached in the early Byzantine
period by taking Matthew 5. 32 as part of the Sermon on the Mount.
It is indeed possible to see the exhortations of the Sermon as the
precepts of an ideal ethic which the Christian, striving after perfection, must try to live up to (and here the Byzantine would first
of all think of monks and nuns), while this would not be asked
of ordinary people. This interpretation is accepted by Roman
Catholicism, the Orthodox Churches and most (though not all)
Protestant Churches in the case of Matthew 5. 34 ("Do not swear
at all").

It is interesting that the interpretation of this precept not to
swear at all occurs several times in Byzantine canonical literature. At the beginning of the section on swearing in the *Basilica*,
the great legal code of Leo the Wise (about A.D. 900), we find
two scholia[10] which contain large extracts from John Chrysostom
(*In Matth*. 17. 5–6 and *De Statuis* 15. 5). Leo himself, in his
Novella 97, argues in a similar way when he compares Matthew
5. 34 with 6. 19 and 25 ("Do not store up treasures for yourselves
on earth" and "Do not worry about your life and what you are
to eat"), texts which, according to him, should not be taken too
literally.

I have not been able to find a direct application of this line of
thought to the question of divorce in sources of Byzantine law,
either secular or ecclesiastical, but this does obviously not mean

---

[10] Bas. 22. 5, *ad rubricam* (ed. Scheltema, ser. B., pp. 1410–1).

that there is no example of it in Byzantine theological literature, which I do not know well enough. I have nevertheless the impression that this argument must have played a part in their broad approach to divorce.

II. REMARRIAGE, ONCE AND SEVERAL TIMES

In Justinian's law there was no restriction on the marriage of a widow or widower. But, as has already been pointed out, the guilty partner in a divorce (or both partners after a divorce by mutual agreement) could not remarry because he or she was compelled to enter a monastery. This sanction, however, was not applied consistently so that in practice this possibility existed in the later period. This sanction was even no longer accepted for a time during the reigns of the iconoclastic emperors who were very hostile to monasticism.

The Greek Fathers interpreted 1 Corinthians 7. 7, 8, 27, 39 and 40 as allowing a second marriage while a third marriage must be punished with a canonical penalty though it remains valid. According to St Basil it is against divine law but better than wholesale fornication. If you marry a fourth time you are behaving like a pig.

This line was pursued in later legislation. Empress Irene[11] forbade the third marriage (about A.D. 800). The emperor Basil[12] allowed a third marriage though with the proviso of an ecclesiastical penalty, but declared a fourth marriage null and void. His son Leo repeated this statement in his 90th *Novella*. But shortly after he did so he married himself for the fourth time, which caused a fierce controversy in the Church. After his death the Synod of Constantinople published in 920 its *Tomos tes henoseos* (Book of Unity)[13] in which fourth marriages were declared null and void while third marriages were allowed under certain conditions. And there the matter still rests.

These regulations were of course applied to widows and widowers. In so far as separated partners are concerned, the only

[11] *Coll. I. Nov.*, 28 (*Ius Graeco-Rom.*, I, p. 49).
[12] *Prochiron 4*, 25 (*Ius Graeco-Rom.*, II, p. 127).
[13] *Coll. II. Nov.*, 1 (*Ius Graeco-Rom.*, I, p. 192). The decree of the Synod was confirmed by the reigning emperors.

thing that is certain is that if the man is ordained bishop or one of the partners enters a monastery, the other partner could marry again. This was accepted in later practice.

The texts do not make it clear what the procedure was in divorces entered upon for other reasons. This is the more curious since, after a decree of Leo the Wise,[14] marriages could only be contracted through the Church's blessing, and no longer outside the Church by mutual agreement in front of witnesses. In all probability princes and notables could no doubt find a priest willing to co-operate with their subsequent marriage if the reason for the divorce was the misbehaviour of the other partner.

[14] *Nov. Leonis*, 89.

Translated by Theo Westow

Philippe Delhaye

The Development of the Medieval Church's Teaching on Marriage

THE Church acquired exclusive control over marriage in the eleventh century. That epoch saw the beginning of the crystallization of canon law teaching on marriage and of the idea of marriage as a sacrament in the proper sense of the word and no longer simply as "something sacred". Up till then people had mostly let themselves be guided pragmatically by the Scriptures and the Fathers.

The Old Testament was concerned with marriage in society (the family as the basic unit) and with the conditions necessary for its proper fulfilment. Moreover, this period of the Middle Ages often looked to the Old Testament for inspiration, for example with regard to the impurities referred to in Leviticus. The New Testament demanded the restoration of the original ideal and emphasized the unity and indissolubility of the marriage bond.

As for the Fathers of the Church, their concern at first was for the moral value of marriage and a host of questions affecting the State, an approach which was probably responsible for numerous errors resulting in numerous heresies ranging from the strictest rigorism to the greatest laxity. St Jerome refuted some of them with his customary vigour, while St Augustine "moralized" more or less exclusively.

On the other hand, during its first thousand years, the Church often had to rest content with merely defending the principles of Christian marriage, when the Roman and then the barbarian invaders' laws had drastically reduced its say in legislative and judiciary affairs. In some areas (Germany, England) certain cases of divorce were allowed, for example by the Penitential Books.

In the course of the struggles between clergy and the empire, the limits to the Church's influence fixed by the civil authorities were gradually removed by the steady increase in ecclesiastical power.

Until then there had been a system of collaboration and sharing or rivalry between the Church and the Christian States, on the subject of marriage; now the weakening of the latter meant that they lost their powers of jurisdiction over marriage, which was henceforth considered a uniquely sacred affair.

Of course this victory on the part of the ecclesiastical authorities was not universal: there were still places in the eleventh century where matrimonial questions were judged by lay tribunals, but these cases were exceptional and gradually ceased.

We can therefore say that the exclusive competence of the Church in matrimonial matters came to be universally accepted in the eleventh century.

In France the weakening of royal power made this transfer from civil to ecclesiastical jurisdiction relatively easy. In Italy it seems that the emperor's habit of conceding civic titles and the corresponding civil powers to numerous bishops had already prepared the way for the exclusive competence of the bishops in matters affecting marriage. In England, finally, where the political situation had evolved somewhat differently, this exclusive competence of ecclesiastical tribunals in matrimonial questions appears to be accepted at the beginning of the twelfth century.

From this time on the Church alone possessed competence in judiciary questions, and she also possessed the power to legislate, to fix the rules governing marriage and to apply her own law in place of the secular laws which she had allowed. She was to be capable of formulating a whole matrimonial code of law.

But very varied customs and legislation were to be found in the Christian world at that time: in order to stabilize the laws affecting marriage and to reach some sort of unity in legislation, the Church had to take account of Roman law, for example, by establishing as valid a marriage freely contracted between the two spouses even when there was no official ceremony.

Marriage was not universally accepted as a sacrament until mid-twelfth century. Sacrament is here used, obviously, in the sense in which the scholastics were to define it between 1140 and 1150—namely a rite which both symbolizes and effects grace, of which they listed seven instances. The sacredness of Christian marriage was of course recognized from earliest times but no one dreamt of translating the *mysterion* referred to in the Epistle to the Ephesians (5. 32) by "sacrament" in the scholastic and Tridentine sense. What is there described as mysterious is the mystical bond between Christ and the Church. The mystery *par excellence*, in the captivity epistles, is God's plan to save all men by identifying them with his Son. Evidently it remains true that the carnal union between man and woman also implies total dedication, a definitive choice, but nobody in the early Church dreamt of going beyond comparisons or moral duties. Moreover, the Middle Ages almost unanimously accepted the notion of sacrament put forward by St Isidore of Seville (*Etymologiae*, I.VI, c. 19, no. 40–42), namely a mysterious presence of the Holy Spirit. Naturally from that point of view, the dogmas of faith as well as all the liturgical acts (even those of the Old Testament) were all sacraments. The eucharistic controversies and advances in theological concepts based on Aristotelian logic led the authors of the *Summa Sententiarum* (Otto of Lucca?) and the *Sententiarum Libri IV* (Peter Lombard) to formulas in which the idea of efficacy was added to the idea of a sign giving the formula we have now and thereby establishing the traditional seven sacraments.

For a long time theologians were uncertain. Ivo of Chartres considered that marriage was not sacramental if the love of charity was lacking between the spouses. Hugh of Amiens held that second marriages could not be sacramental because they could not signify the unique and definitive love of Christ for his Church. Hugh of St Victor distinguished between the *sacramentum conjugii* and the *sacramentum conjugalis officii*. The first, *maius sacramentum*, symbolized the union between God and the soul; the second, *magnum sacramentum*, symbolized the union of Christ and the Church. In the *Decretum* of Gratian, as in the works of its innumerable commentators, the word sacrament applied to marriage could mean either the indissolubility of the marriage bond or the bond itself or its mystical significance. Around 1150, as one can observe in the *Sentences* of Peter Lombard especially, the list of the seven sacraments was becoming established: *"baptismus, confirmatio, panis bene-dictionis, id est eucharistia, poenitentia, extrema unctio, ordo, coniugium"* (Book 4, Dist. 2) paving the way towards a *"de sacra-mentis"* of a type which was novel then but which has since been classical and official.

For a long time in the twelfth century uncertainty persisted as regards which element essentially constituted marriage: consent or *copula*?

This problem was posed again and again, and the argument bitterly contested, for various reasons. Roman law, which was undergoing a revival, based marriage on the consent of the spouses: *"consensus facit nuptias"* (Ulpian, *Digest.*, I, 17, 30, and *Cod. Justin.*, V, 17, 8). Many of the Fathers, notably St Leo, de-fended this point of view, as Peter Lombard points out (*Sentences,* Book 4, Dist. 27). But on the other hand German custom re-quired *copula* in recognizing the existence of the marriage bond. Another consideration involved was the marriage between Joseph and Mary: it would be reduced to nothing if *copula* was a pre-requisite *ad validitatem*. Finally, there were the examples of the saints (Alexis was often cited) and the *praxis Ecclesiae*: the latter permitted a girl married by her relatives to enter a religious order without the consent of the husband if the latter had not consum-mated the marriage.

Ivo of Chartres required only consent and considered *copula* unnecessary. However, in a somewhat illogical way, the great authority on canon law also taught that *copula* was an added complement to the reality of the bond. Abelard and Hugh of St Victor rejected the idea put forward by the school of Laon that the marriage existed from the time of consent but only became "perfect" when it was consummated. Nevertheless something along these lines was to find its way into the *Decretum* of Gratian and the works of the canon lawyers. The *matrimonium initiatum* was brought about by the consent of the spouses. The *matri-monium ratum* alone was perfect and required *copula* (*consum-matum*). To avoid saying that the marriage between Joseph and

Mary was imperfect, Gratian launched into mystical considerations. He set much store by the distinction between *sponsi* (who consented mutually) and *conjugii* (who had intercourse), and based numerous conclusions on it concerning entering the religious life, the effect of impotence on the validity of a marriage, *divortium*, second marriages.

Gratian's thesis was generally accepted in Italy, and Peter Lombard's in France. Alexander III and Innocent III only partially rallied to the latter, which had to await the *Decretals* of Gregory IX before finally carrying the day. Indeed the popes were occasionally confronted with the case known as *sponsa duorum*: a woman who had accepted a husband in that she had pronounced the words of the marriage rite, but who had subsequently contracted marriage with another man with mutual consent and consummation of the marriage. Alexander III was manifestly hesitant on this point and only accepted the validity of the first marriage if the words of engagement had been said in the presence of a notary or a priest. And even so he admitted his difficulty in the face of the arguments of theologians and canon lawyers. He opted for the side which seemed to him to be the more certain.

Marriage was often depreciated and considered an inferior state of life. There were limits to this tendency, however, inspired by fear of appearing to sympathize with the remnants of Manicheism.

Lucien Febvre once wrote that for medieval man marriage was a "sacrament of tolerance". It is difficult not to share this view when one reads the texts of the time, for example the *Sentences* of Peter Lombard which were studied and commented upon in the schools for four hundred years. Sexual intercourse was to be excused by the goods brought about by marriage, beginning with procreation (Book 4, Dist. 32, Chapter 5). If it was sought as a means of satisfying desire it constituted a venial sin according to the teaching of St Augustine. The spouses were thus in practice considered to be sinners. They were warned against too ardent a love for each other in the name of Sextus the Pythagorean's precept which was everywhere held up to them: *"omnis ardentior amator propriae uxoris, adulter est"*. Sexual pleasure was not always formally sinful but it was bad all the same. St Gregory advised that one should abstain from attending liturgical offices after having given way to it (*Sent.*, Book 4, Dist. 32, Chapter 8).

Alongside these "moderate" trends there existed more radical movements which went back via the Bogomiles to Manicheism and Masdaism. As far as these were concerned bodily life was essentially evil; to transmit it was to collaborate with the evil one. Thus marriage was absolutely condemned for the *élite* of the sect. If necessary initiation into this state of perfection could be put off till shortly before death in order to avoid the risk of returning to a sexual life. The twelfth century saw the proliferation of this "little church", and in a variety of different guises: Albigenses (Cathari) and Waldenses were very similar in this respect in spite of the fact that their starting-points were very different. The polemic directed against these people was to point to a revaluation of marriage among Catholics. This is especially evident in the case of Alain of Lille, the professor at Paris and later at Montpellier, who joined the Cistercians in the early days of the Catholic counter-offensive. Periodically councils recalled men to the respect due to marriage: Lateran Council II (Denzinger 718), Verona (Denzinger 761), Lateran IV (Denzinger 802). The retractation demanded of the Waldensian converts (taking Waldensian in its wider sense) by Innocent III was equally explicit (Denzinger 794).

Translated by Jonathan Cavanagh

Piet Fransen

Divorce on the Ground of Adultery—The Council of Trent (1563)

IN this article I want to summarize the main arguments and conclusions worked out in previous studies of canon 7.[1] On this basis I will then give a commentary on the text of this canon. The main references to the sources are put in brackets in the text.[2]

The Council of Trent dealt twice with the question of marriage: first, after it had moved to Bologna at the end of the second period, from April to November 1547 (VI 96–578), and then sixteen years later at Trent under Pius IV, from 4 February to 11 November 1563 (IX 380–977 and III 566–750). The dogmatic bearing of canon 7 was only decided in 1563 because of the procedure followed in Trent. The discussions that took place in Bologna are nevertheless useful for an understanding of certain formulas embodied in the canon.

[1] P. Fransen, "Die Formel 'si quis dixerit ecclesiam errare' im Kanon 6 und 8 der 24. Sitzung des Trienter Konzils", in *Scholastik*, 25 (1950), pp. 492–517; "Die Formel 'si quis dixerit ecclesiam errare' und ähnliche Ausdrücke bei der Beratung des 4. und anderer Kanones der 24. Sitzung des Trienter Konzils", in *Scholastik*, 26 (1951), pp. 191–221; "Ehescheidung im Fall von Ehebruch. Der Fundamental-dogmatischer Ertrag der Bologneser Verhandlungen, 1547", in *Scholastik*, 27 (1952), pp. 526–56; "Réflexions sur l'anathème au Concile de Trente (Bologne, 10–24 septembre 1547)", in *Ephem. Theol. Lov.*, 29 (1953), pp. 657–72; "Echtscheiding na echtbreuk van een van de gehuwden. Het kerkrechterlijk dossier van Trente (1563)", in *Bijdragen*, 14 (1953), pp. 363–87; "Ehescheidung bei Ehebruch", in *Scholastik*, 29 (1954), pp. 537–60 and 30 (1955), pp. 33–50.

[2] The Roman numerals refer to the volumes of the Görres edition, *Concilium Tridentinum* (Freiburg); CI refers to *Corpus Iuris*, ed. Friedberg, I (Leipzig); Calini refers to Muzio Calini, *Lettere conciliari* (1561–1563)

89

I. The Main Arguments

1. Luther's Position

In his *De captivitate babylonica,* to which Trent mainly refers, Luther's position was not yet clear. He was, however, quite clear on the point "that this issue could not be decided by the Pope or the bishops".[3] The Roman Church had therefore acted "like a tyrant", that is, had exceeded its competence. The formulation of the canon remained clumsy and unwieldy because the Council wanted to follow the procedure laid down at Trent and quote Luther himself as his opinion had been summarized on 16 April 1547 (VI 98–99), even though the Commission had proposed a juridically more precise formula on 18 October 1547 (VI 537, 9).

2. The Interpretation of Scripture by the Church

The attitude of the theologians and bishops at the Council may be described as follows. Most of them stuck to Augustine's interpretation of Matthew 5. 32 and 19. 9 (separation of bed and board), although some admitted that these texts of Matthew were not immediately clear. On the other hand, the early Councils (the "sacred canons"), the *Decretum Gratiani,* and the later papal decretals had created a firm legal tradition in the West which rejected any breaking of the marriage bond.[4] So, if necessary, they felt they could take refuge in this legal tradition and uphold it, with an anathema. This was possible in Trent because of the broader sense given to the phrase "defining the faith" (*deffinire fidem*). Such a procedure had already been suggested by Cardinal del Monte in September 1546 (VI 402–407).

3. The Fathers of the Church

There remained, however, a serious difficulty. Some theologians and bishops, better acquainted with patristic literature, were aware of statements made by Origen, Epiphanius, Basil,

---

(Brescia, 1963); Visconti refers to the letters of Carolo Visconti, bishop of Ventimiglia, in Baluze-Mansi, *Miscellanea,* III (Lucca, 1762), pp. 43 ff.

[3] "Tamen in iis nihil definio (ut dixi), quamquam nihil magis optarem esse definitum, cum nihil magis me et multos mecum vexet hodie. Sola auctoritate Papae aut Episcoporum hic diffiniri nihil volo", in *De captivitate babylonica* (*Luthers Werke,* Weimar, VI, p. 560).

[4] Excellently summarized by Pedro de Soto (IX 409–10).

Theodoret and Chrysostom, which did not follow this rigid interpretation. All knew, of course, of the two objections mentioned in *Causa* 32, q. 7, of the *Decretum Gratiani*, which were taken from Ambrose and Gregory (CI 1145–1149). That the quotations from Ambrose were not authentic (Ambrosiaster) was known to only very few before Erasmus. Ambrose was the great Doctor of the West for most bishops, while the text from Gregory II did not refer to adultery and was therefore not often quoted.

Because of this many felt, right at the beginning, that one could not apply the anathema to this case. At the time of Trent the anathema was still quite clearly the equivalent of excommunication, and it was hardly possible to anathematize a Father of the Church. The Commission charged with the drafting of the canons (IX 59, 1–15) produced on 20 July both a draft for a canon with an anathema and a so-called "decree" without an anathema. The latter has been lost. But M. Calini described its purpose on 26 July as follows: "Many bishops have expressed the wish that, instead of a canon, a decree should be drafted stating that it was not permitted (*non fosse lecito*) in such cases (of adultery) to contract a new marriage with other persons" (Calini 502; Visconti 438A and IX 644, 35). In this way the text would be limited to a re-affirmation of that Western legal tradition which has been mentioned above.

4. *The Orthodox East*

On 11 August the Fathers began a second series of discussions of the 6th canon which, amended by the Commission, then became canon 7 (IX 682, 21). But before the bishops had the chance of moving their interventions, the Venetian delegation put forward a demand that the canon be re-drafted in such a way that the anathema would be maintained but the excommunication would not apply to the Fathers of the Church and the Eastern Church. This intervention was immediately backed by Cardinals de Guise and Madruzio of Trent (IX 686, 28–33).

In order to follow the Venetian argument one must understand the peculiar symbiosis which marked the relations between the Latin and Greek communities in the territories ruled by Venice, particularly on the islands of the Mediterranean. The local bishops were usually Venetians of the Latin rite. But their clergy were largely Orthodox and under the authority of a *protopapas*. The Latin bishops let their people and lower clergy live by the Orthodox tradition. The clergy were allowed to seek ordination from Orthodox bishops on the continent as long as they had obtained *litterae dimissoriales* from the Latin bishop. The bishops only stipulated that three times a year all the people should publicly recognize the authority of the Pope by the recitation of the so-called *Laudes*.[5]

Rome and the bishops at the Council seem to have tolerated this colonial compromise, with only few exceptions. They were under the impression that in this way Venice had achieved ecclesial unity and that the "rite" was the only difference between Greeks and Latins. Since the whole context shows that this difference in rite had a far deeper meaning at that time than today, we are forced to give a broader meaning to *"ritus"* at the Council. In practice, divorce after adultery was counted as part of this difference in "rite".

5. *A Peculiarity in the Formulation of the Canon*

We must also briefly point out the peculiar formulation of the canon: *"Si quis dixerit ecclesiam errare ..."* (if anyone says that the Church errs...). This phrase is also found in other canons of this session.[6] This is a clever formula which ensured that the anathema and excommunication pointed exclusively to the statements made by the Reformers that in its juridical practice the Church had, in a "tyrannical way", exceeded its competence in the matter of divorce. I have already shown above that Luther had stated his position clearly only on this particular point. The word *"errare"* must therefore be understood in this sense.

6. *The Council of Florence*

Another argument emerged from the discussion, namely, that

[5] G. Hoffmann, "Wie stand es mit der Frage der Kircheneinheit auf Kreta im XV. Jahrhundert?" in *Orientalia Christ. Periodica*, 10 (1946), pp. 91–115.

[6] See note 1, the first two articles. This form of condemnation was attacked as ambiguous right up to the end by a minority, and principally by G. Drascovics, bishop of Fünfkirchen (Pécs) (IX 903, 39 and 975, 26).

when the Council of Florence dealt with the question of union with the Greeks, it had not touched on this particular question (Foscarari: III, 692, 2, and especially Bovio, bishop of Ostuni: IX 723, 40–724, 2). Against this other bishops brought up the *Decretum pro Armenis*, published by the same Council, where the only possibility of divorce is stated to be separation of board and bed (Denz. 702 or Denz.–Schönm. 1327).

In actual fact, Eugene IV had tried, after the solemn proclamation of the bull of unity and the Emperor had already left Rome, to solve this problem with the Greeks who were still in Rome. But these declared themselves incompetent to deal with this question (Harduinus IX 430–431).[7]

7. Political Pressure

We now have the main arguments brought forward in the discussions preparatory to Trent. These were only dogmatic arguments. But in Trent this dogmatic labour was also weighed down by international politics, such as the powerful pressure exercised by the Spanish bishops who were charged by Philip II to put a brake on the hurry with which Pius IV wished to bring the Council to its conclusion. Although these factors indirectly influenced the discussions I cannot deal with them here. But it is curious, for instance, to see how, in the second half of 1563, the Spanish bishops put forward objections, and this in both directions, to a more rigid and to a more accommodating formulation of the canon.

II. COMMENTARY ON THE TEXT OF CANON 7

Si quis dixerit Ecclesiam errare (If anyone says that the Church errs).

Errare. In the nineteenth century and at the beginning of this one, when controversy raged about papal infallibility, several encyclopedias and textbooks took this as a straight definition of the Church's infallibility in matters of Church law about marriage. But the whole ideological context of the sixteenth century, particularly in the controversies connected with Luther, shows

---

[7] J. Gill, *The Council of Florence* (Cambridge, 1959), p. 297.

that this word has a broader meaning, namely, "to exceed one's competence", even though it does not exclude the idea of doctrinal error.

Cum docuit et docet, iuxta evangelicam et apostolicam doctrinam (when it has taught and still teaches, according to the doctrine of the gospel and the apostles). On 5 September the Commission had omitted the word *docet*. At the insistence of Cardinal de Guise it was put back. Loyal to their Gallican tradition, Cardinal de Guise and the French bishops wanted to emphasize the teaching of the old councils, that of Elvira (Mansi II, 7) and particularly that of Milevis. At Trent it was commonly thought that Augustine had taken part in this last one and that it had been approved by Innocent I. In actual fact, the quotation from Gratian in c. 5, C. 32, qu. 7, refers to the 11th provincial Council of Carthage in 407. The beginning of this quotation is, however, important for the formulation of our canon 7: *"Placuit ut secundum evangelicam et apostolicam disciplinam..."* (CI 1141; Harduinus I 1222 sub 17).

Gratian himself used this formula repeatedly in this Causa 32 and 33. This is clearest where he rejects the argument based on the text taken from Gregory II: "This saying of Gregory has been found to be wholly contrary to the sacred canons, and *even* (*immo*) to the teaching of the gospel and the apostles" (In C. 32, qu. 7, IV, par. 1; CI 1145; see also C. 33, qu. 1; CI 1148–9).

The "evangelical teaching" refers to the gospels, obviously including Matthew, while "apostolical" probably refers to Paul. Both Gratian and the bishops at Trent clearly distinguish these two sources from the sacred canons of the early Councils which built up the canonical tradition. We should not forget that the old law was common or customary law, mainly based on pronouncement by Councils, popes and bishops.

"When it has taught and still teaches" refers, therefore, to the historical fact that these sacred canons and the papal decretals taught the indissolubility of marriage, and continue to do so.

Iuxta (according to) is important here, particularly when we compare this formulation with the way in which Gratian used the phrase *evangelica et apostolica disciplina*. Gratian *identified* the teaching of the sacred canons with the teaching of the gospel and the apostles. The Council wanted to leave this question formally open.

This appears most clearly in the observation made by Andrés Questa, bishop of León, member of the Commission in charge of the drafting of the canons, who therefore knew the real bearing of the 7th canon from the work done by the Commission. He remained opposed to the Venetian proposal. On 9 September he still maintained that "The canon should be kept as first drafted, or the text should be written as: *Si quis dixerit ecclesiam errare cum evangelicam et apostolicam doctrinam docuit et docet"* (IX 789, 27; and again on 26 October: IX 903, 42). What the Church has taught and still teaches is therefore identical with what is taught by the gospel and Paul.

Martín Pérez de Ayala, bishop of Segovia, and N. G. Nogueras, bishop of Alife, favoured another interpretation. They wanted a text which was more definitely in favour of the Oriental Church (IX 785, 33 and 793, 31), and the canon should read: "If anyone says that the Church errs and teaches something beyond (*praeter*) the teaching of the gospel and the apostles. . . ." The reason de Ayala gives for this is that "In this canon it is said that this 'dogma' is *derived from* Scripture (*habetur ex Scriptura*), which is not evident" (IX 785, 33).

The Council rejected both proposals. It did not want to declare formally that this "teaching" was identical with the teaching of Scripture, nor simply affirm that this teaching was not against or beyond that of Scripture. The first declaration would imply that the Council took up a definite stand on a point about which there was controversy among Catholics, something which Trent tried to avoid as far as possible. The second would imply that the Council was satisfied with a minimal declaration that the teaching of the sacred canons did not go against or beyond Scripture.

The word *iuxta* expresses a medium position between these two extremes. This teaching of the sacred canons was *inspired* by Scripture. The Council left biblical scholars free to explain in more detail what exactly the bond was which linked the canonical tradition with the teaching of Scripture.

Propter adulterium alterius coniugum matrimonii vinculum

non posse dissolvi (that the bond of marriage cannot be dissolved by the adultery of one of the partners).

At the start of the proceedings, on 20 July, the Commission's draft simply read "that the marriage cannot be dissolved" (IX 640, 12). The more detailed phrase "the bond of marriage" only came in on 13 October.

This correction is important. The canon only deals with what the textbooks call the "intrinsic indissolubility" of marriage, namely, that a marriage does not *ipso facto* break up because of adultery, or, in terms that come closer to Luther's thought in his *De captivitate babylonica,* with the fact that the partners decide this question among themselves in their own conscience. The Council made no statement about whether it was possible for the Church itself to declare a divorce. This aspect of the question would, according to the textbooks, come under the heading of "extrinsic (in)dissolubility".

The Council could have taken this line because Luther had made it quite plain that, in his view, neither Pope nor bishops would be competent to do so. In this case the Council would have involved the Eastern Church in its anathema, but neither does that Church accept that this is merely a matter for the personal decision of the partners.

This is why, already in 1547, the discussion quite clearly took a different turn. With reference to the two quotations from Luther (VI 98–99) the canon relates adultery very closely with divorce, as the Commission made clear when it noted that "the woman would cease to be a wife, ... *in order* to contract a new marriage" (*adeo* uxor esse desiit, ... *ut* liceat novare coniugium) (VI 402, 20; 407, 12 and 446, 7).

In 1563 this rigid connection was abandoned. But the thought behind it remained implied. And this was precisely the reason for the change of *matrimonium* into *matrimonii vinculum.* It is also clear from the structure of the canon which continues immediately with *"et utrumque coniugum ... non posse".* Thus the anathema applied only to Luther's position and not to the Eastern Church.

Et utrumque coniugum, vel saltem innocentem, qui causam adulterii non dedit, non posse, altero coniuge vivente, aliud matrimonium contrahere, moecharique eum qui dimissa adultera alteram duxerit, et eam, quae dimisso adultero, alii nupserit (and that neither partner, not even the innocent one who has not committed adultery, can, while the other partner is alive, contract another marriage; both he that leaves the adulterous wife and takes another, and she that leaves the adulterous husband and gives herself to another in marriage, commit adultery).

There is not much to be said about this part. It is easy to see why this canon is so long-winded. The Council simply wanted to embody the two quotations from Luther, as summarized by the Commission in 1547, almost verbally, in order to make clear that the anathema referred exclusively and formally to the teaching of the Reformation. It did not aim formally at the person of Luther, because Trent did not want to hit at particular persons, but only at specific doctrines.

Vel saltem innocentem. The preferential treatment of the innocent party was known to Luther, to Eastern canon law and to most of the conciliar Fathers.

One more point. During the discussions about the teaching of the Fathers of Church and the older canonical traditions some bishops had become aware of the fact that the old law showed more tolerance for the man than for the woman. This was clearly the situation in the Old Testament. We would therefore expect that some of this long-standing discrimination would have spilled over in the treatment of this question at Trent. It is the more interesting that the Council did not yield to this social pressure and explicitly treated both man and woman in the same way.

Anathema sit.

Both Cardinal del Monte, papal legate to the Council in 1547, and the Commission itself in 1563, asked in so many words whether the anathema was really wanted here. Del Monte argued that the question had been already canonically decided (VI 402, 7–14), and therefore no longer left any doubt in law. The Commission of 1563 did not want to anathematize, let alone excommunicate, "Ambrose and the others".

In the end the Council maintained the anathema, both at Bologna and Trent, because it wanted to determine a "dogma" by attaching the penalty of excommunication to the teaching of the Reformers.

Others have dealt in detail with the meaning of "dogma", *"fides"* and *"haeresis"* at the time of the Council of Trent.[8] There is no room for this here. But this canon provides us with a good example of what was meant by "dogma" at Trent. It is not necessarily about a truth directly revealed by God, as Vatican I was to define it after three centuries of theological reflection.

The content of this canon 7 is clearly the content of the *docuit et docet*, seen in the context of the sacred canons, i.e., the existing legal tradition in the Western Church. This teaching, however, is not seen merely as a canonical decision, in which case a "decree" would have been enough according to the terminology current at Trent. It is therefore seen as an element of Church order which goes further than a simple juridical norm, because it touches the structure of the sacramental ministry in the Church and is inspired by (*iuxta*) Scripture. Finally, this practice and this teaching were universally accepted in the Western Church, and this, too, is an element of "dogma".

One final question. Does the anathema affect the practice of the Oriental Church? The whole trend of the discussion shows that only a negative answer to this question fits in with the facts of history. There is not the slightest doubt that Trent accepted the proposal of the Venetians who definitely wanted to avoid an excommunication of the Easterns and a possible threat to the fragile and rather superficial ecclesiastical unity which existed in their territories in the East.

The bishops of Cyprus reaffirmed this at the solemn session of 11 November and had it put on record by the secretary to the Council who embodied it in the *Acta*. Filippo Mocenigo, archbishop of Nicosia and primate of Cyprus, read out a confession of faith from a provincial Council of 1340, held by the then primate, Elias de Nabidalis, O.Min., in which the Greek, Maronite and Armenian communities recognized the Church of Rome as the "mother and teacher of all the faithful" and accepted the primacy of the Pope.

---

[8] A. Lang, "Der Bedeutungswandel der Begriffe 'fides' und 'haeresis' und die dogmatische Wertung der Konzilsentscheidungen von Vienne und Trient", in *Münchener Theol. Zeits.*, 4 (1953), pp. 133–46; P. Fransen, "Enkele bemerkingen over de theologische kwalificaties", in *Tijds. voor Theologie*, 8 (1968), pp. 328–47.

It is significant that the Venetian delegation used these words from that confession of faith in their amendment to the canon. It is more than probable that in all this the Venetian bishops and ambassadors worked together. In this profession of faith the Greeks and others had asked "that they be allowed to continue to live according to their rites (*in suis ritibus*) which do not deviate from the faith" (IX, 972, 3–10). This, too, was mentioned in the address given by the Venetian delegation.

The Primate was supported by the other bishops of Cyprus, Andrea Mocenigo of Limasol (IX 976, 46), Girolamo Raggazini of Famagusta (IX 977, 4) and Francesco Contarini, bishop of Baffo (Paphos) (IX 977, 33). This declaration was officially recorded in the Acts, which proves that the Council accepted it as such.

This is shown by a small incident that occurred on 11 August. M. Calini said in his letter of 12 August that the Venetian Pietro Landi, bishop of Candia in Crete, had stated that "the Greeks should not be condemned without being given the opportunity to explain their attitude. It was therefore appropriate that they should first be called together and invited to speak" (Calini 512).

At first the Legates ignored this. When some bishops repeated the complaint that the Greeks had not been invited to the Council, the second President, Cardinal Hosius, bishop of Ermland in East Prussia, intervened to say that the Greeks and the Russians had in fact been invited.[9] The Venetian delegation must have mentioned this, too. Thus Carlo Visconti, the confidential agent of the Legates, wrote in the letter where he dealt with the incident in detail: "And after the meal the Legates ordered the Secretary to erase the words '*non fuerint*' from the petition of the Venetian delegation" (Visconti 488B).

In the Acts, too, there is no trace left of the complaint made by Pietro Landi and the other bishops, apart from the protest by the archbishop of Prague (IX 698, 27). All that is left of Pietro Landi's argument is: "*probavi pluribus rationibus*" (I proved this with several arguments) (IX 688, 25–29). This holds also for the text of the petition presented by the Venetian delegation as it has been preserved in the Acts (IX 686, 3–37, with note 3).

[9] W. de Vries, "Einladung nicht-römisch-katholischer Orientalen zum Konzil von Trient", in *Catholica*, 15 (1961), pp. 134–50.

A protest by a bishop or group of bishops or delegates is only recorded in the Acts when the Legates and the Council agree with it. This happened with the statement of the bishops of Cyprus that the Eastern Christians should be allowed "to live according to their rites".

Translated by Theo Westow

Denis O'Callaghan

Marriage as Sacrament

THE theology of marriage has had a particularly difficult history. It suffered at the hands of both the moralist and the canonist while the systematic theologian tended to stand aloof.[1] The pastoral considerations of educating for marriage and of developing a spirituality of marriage have occasioned a good deal of progress in recent years, even though the birth-control controversy, a controversy all the more bitter in that it is the maelstrom where old and new theological currents meet, has tended to polarize debate on what is essentially a side issue.

One should not wonder that it took twelve centuries or more to achieve general recognition of marriage as sacrament. The distrust of the body and its senses, the tendency to identify the concupiscence of fallen man with sexual passion, the need to extol virginity, all these prejudiced marriage. In addition, the contractual approach favoured by canon law was a barrier to theological progress. The canonist provided a totally unsatisfactory and impoverished definition of the object of consent by expressing it in terms of an exchange of physical sexual rights,[2] and his preoccupation with the permanence of the marriage bond distracted

---

[1] For the history of marriage in the Church see P. Adnès, *Le Mariage* (Coll. Le Mystère Chrétien (Tournai, 1961); J. E. Kerns, *The Theology of Marriage* (The Historical Development of Christian Attitudes towards Sex and Sanctity in Marriage) (New York, 1964); E. Schillebeeckx, *Marriage, Secular Reality and Saving Mystery* (London, 1965) (*Het Huwelijk: aardse werkelijkheid en heilsmysterie* [Bilthoven, 1963]).

[2] "Le droit canonique assigne aux rapports sexuels, à la *copula carnalis*, une importance particulière; aucune autre legislation, je le crois, n'est

from the far more important question of the nature and quality of the marriage relationship.

From the systematic theologian's viewpoint the theology of the sacrament was further crippled in that marriage did not seem to conform to the typical sacramental structure. Where was the Church's official minister?—practice made it clear that the presence and blessing of a priest was not essential. Where was the ritual sacramental sign?—there was no special sacral gesture set aside for this purpose, nothing except the commonplace coming together in marriage of Christian man and woman.

These were problems for the systematic theologian, but these very problems were the key to the sacramental nature of marriage. Marriage does not need to be ritualized. The secular reality itself is transformed into a sanctifying and redeeming force and there is no need to add anything from outside. It shares in Christ's redemptive mission in the Church because it commits man and woman to one another and to life together precisely as Christians. Given the limitations of the system, theology expressed this insight in the formula: "Every matrimonial contract between Christians is a sacrament." Even though a good deal of the traditional insistence on this principle was politically coloured in that it was directed against those who campaigned for State control over the marriage contract, and even though its suggestion of automatic sacramentality raised insurmountable difficulties in the field of sacramental intention, it was a real insight, and it is by developing this that our theology of marriage has grown.

The step which promises most for the sacramental theology of marriage is the change of emphasis from marriage-contract to marriage-institution. This is not just a question of methodology. It is much more. It gives far greater content to the concept of sacrament and situates its theology far more solidly and comprehensively. It should be remarked that Vatican II in its Constitution *On the Church in the Modern World* constantly refers to marriage in terms of community (*communitas coniugalis et*

entrée aussi loin dans cette voie"—Esmein-Genestal, *Le mariage en droit canonique*, vol. 1 (Paris, 1929), p. 89. Sanchez stated that the marriage due was more binding than any property right, and there was no need to go to court to extort it—*De Matrimonio*, lib. 2, disp. 22, n. 13.

familiaris, communitas vitae et amoris) and institution (*matri-moniale familiareque institutum*). The term *contract* is not used, and where one would expect such mention the more biblical and theological word *covenant* (*foedus matrimoniale*) occurs.

Of course, it was always taken for granted that there was an institution of marriage which specified and standardized the consent and identified it formally as marital consent. Canon law had this institutional background in mind when it referred to marriage as a perpetual and exclusive union, as an association of man and woman for specific purposes.[3] But all this was twisted to suit the contractual approach. To describe marriage formally as an institution declares that it is something which exists in its own right as an established reality prior to any compact by the partners, that it reaches back to the very roots of man's life and experience and is material for study by all the human sciences rather than an object of positive legislation. In their consent husband and wife accept not just one another but this whole way of life. The consent can be defined only in terms of the institution since this gives it its full content and depth of meaning.

The concept of institution is all the more important in that it includes in its scope that complex reality which is sacramental marriage, marriage in Christian terms. The theology of Christian marriage is complex because it is something which belongs to both the secular and the sacred, the order of creation and the order of redemption. It is only in terms of the whole institution that the sacrament can be explained and made real. Here the divine and the Christian transfuse and transform the human and the natural.

As a human institution marriage associates man and woman in a family unit in which they achieve their identity and fulfilment and rear new life to responsible adulthood in an atmosphere of loving communion. As a Christian institution marriage is a sacramental and consecrated state in which the various elements of natural wedlock are given a redeeming force and are directed towards the realization of the Kingdom of God. Against this background marriage consent is the dedication of man and woman in partnership to a Christian mission in Church and world. On these terms their consent is properly called marriage vow.

[3] Cc. 1013, 1082, 1110.

The key to the sacramental nature of marriage is to see it as a man-woman relationship directed to integrate and perfect the partners as persons and as Christians, to procreate and develop new human persons and new Christians, and eventually to civilize and Christianize the world at large. Indeed, the cold word *institution* may tend to reify and freeze what is essentially a personal relationship, but this will be true of any technical term.

The relationship of husband and wife is not that of one against the other, a tension characteristic of justice, but of both together, a union characteristic of love. When Vatican II defined marriage as a community of love it effectively endorsed the view of those theologians (particularly Herbert Doms) who claimed that love was not something to be forced in among the so-called secondary purposes of marriage. The community of love, the two-in-oneness of the partners is not just a purpose of marriage, it is the very essence of the marriage institution. This is what marriage *is* in its own right before *being for* anything. It is hard to understand that what passed as valid definitions of marriage in the later manual tradition could have omitted all reference to love, or even to community of life. This came from accepting that the object of consent as described by canon law was the essence of marriage. At least the Scholastic definition[4] took over from Roman law the concept of a two-in-one way of life (*individua vitae consuetudo*), but the possibilities of this were not developed.

It is this relationship, conjugal and parental, which Christ grasps and sanctifies in the sacrament of marriage. The manual tradition tended to ritualize the sacrament and to centre too much on the moment of consent, whereas the whole sacramental meaning of this comes from the sacramental relationship which it initiates. Marriage is a permanent sacrament, not in the sense that the married relationship continues and perpetuates the sacramental force of the consent, but in the sense that this relationship is the sacrament first and foremost and in its own right. Pius XI quoted the words of Cardinal Bellarmine:

The sacrament of marriage may be considered in two ways; in the moment of its accomplishment and in its permanency

[4] Peter Lombard, IV, *Sentient.*, D. 27, c. 2; S. Thomas, *Suppl.*, q. 44, a. 3.

afterwards. This sacrament, in fact, is similar to the Eucharist, which likewise is a sacrament not only in the moment of its accomplishment, but also as long as it remains. For as long as husband and wife live their association is always the sacrament of Christ and of the Church.[5]

This is nothing more than the theological development of the Pauline teaching of Ephesians, chapter 5, a teaching which is basic for any theology of the sacrament. For St Paul the relationship of Christian husband and wife reflects and makes visible the vital exchange of life and love which makes Christ one with his bride, the Church. Christian marriage takes its place in that living and life-giving union and becomes a force in the mission of redemption. St Paul finds the real meaning of marriage in its function and significance in the Mystical Body: "This is a great sacrament, and I take it to refer to Christ and the Church."[6] Here he speaks not of symbol but of reality. He means that Christian marriage is inserted into the sphere of the redemption, that the fundamental mystery of Christianity, the fruitful unity between Christ and the Church, is realized anew in every Christian marriage. It is from this source that he draws his picture of the moral attitudes which should inspire Christian marriage and of the loyalty and fidelity which should characterize it—husband and wife are united not because they are of one bone and one flesh, but because they are members of the one body of Christ: "Because we are members of his body. For this reason a man shall leave his father and mother and be joined to his wife, and the two shall become one."[7]

Every relationship is unique because of the individual persons and situations involved, and every relationship waxes and wanes. Suppose the relationship ceases to have human meaning, suppose love dies so that man and woman come to live under the one roof as strangers or as enemies, or decide to live apart as single people, does the sacrament cease? The sacrament is not just the relationship as it appears here and now but the relationship as sealed in the formal marriage covenant, just as the sacrament of

---

[5] Bellarmine, *De controversiis*, III (*De matrimonio*), cont. 2, c. 6. *A.A.S.*, 22 (1930), p. 583.
[6] Eph. 5. 32.   [7] Eph. 5. 30–1.

the Eucharist is not just bread and wine as sacrificially consecrated. St Paul states: "A wife is bound to her husband as long
as he lives",[8] and Bellarmine says: "As long as husband and wife
live, their association is always the sacrament of Christ and of
the Church."[9] The bond in virtue of which they are husband and
wife remains and this basis of the human relationship is the sacramental reality (res-sacramentum) of the Christian relationship,
even though it is now an ineffective or dormant sacrament. If
there is guilt or failure on either side the sacrament remains as
a constant reproach but,[10] in any case, it offers the possibility of
reactualization.

The sacramental nature of marriage means that every facet
and aspect of human marriage assumes a supernatural dimension. This is true above all of love. Love becomes charity. Eros,
while retaining all its natural force, becomes agape, the expression of a love which is essentially orientated to God, a love of
two Christians with all that this implies. It is at once creative and
redemptive. It is creative in that its innate force and vitality
come from God and reflect the dynamism of the divine nature.
Man and woman made in God's image, love in God's image.
"God is love; he who abides in love abides in God and God
abides in him."[11] It is redemptive in that it shares in the love by
which Christ loves and redeems the Church. "Husbands, love
your wives as Christ loved the Church, and gave himself up for
her that he might sanctify her."[12] This love of Christ is total and
faithful: total, in that he gave his life for his beloved; faithful,
in that nothing can separate her from the love of Christ.

Church law has been particularly interested in the parallel between the love of Christ and the Church and the love of Christian
husband and wife on the supposition that the fidelity of the former may argue the indissolubility of the latter. It is taught that
this mystical symbolism indicates that consummated sacramental
marriage cannot be dissolved. The Pauline text is certainly

---

[8] 1 Cor. 7. 39.   [9] Loc. cit.

[10] "It remains to increase the guilt of the crime, not to strengthen the
bond of alliance; just as the soul of an apostate who deserts his commitment to Christ, does not lose, even after losing his faith, the sacrament of
faith which he received in baptism"—St Augustine, De nuptiis et con-
cupiscentia, 1, 1, 10 (PL 44, 420).

[11] 1 John 4. 15.   [12] Eph. 5. 25-6.

important in the debate, but it is hardly permissible to read it as an absolute legal imperative. Legal dispensation and dissolution are quite outside Paul's interest here. He speaks a different language, the language of sacramental sign-value. He speaks of the quality of the marriage relationship and of the attitudes which should inspire it rather than of the permanence of the bond. "As the Church is subject to Christ, so let wives also be subject in everything to their husbands"[13]—should this also be taken as an absolute legal imperative, valid at all times and places?

The love which Christ has grasped and made his own as a redeeming force in Christian marriage finds expression in the varied opportunities of family life. Every sign of affection between husband and wife is an expression of the will to communicate the life of Christ to the other and is the actual communication of that life. If "the unbelieving husband is consecrated through his wife and the unbelieving wife is consecrated through her husband",[14] how much more true is this of Christian husband and Christian wife?

Love is incarnated in bodily and material gesture. This bodiliness and materiality is not just the outward expression of a spiritual reality independent and complete in itself, as if human love were something essentially spiritual and interior. The body is not something man has, it is something man is. So, Christian married love is a sanctifying force in all its forms, from the most spiritual to the most physical. Marriage in its entirety is restored to God. This is what one means when one speaks of the married relationship as sacramental. The effort to live a genuinely married life, the expressions of love and affection, the acts of consideration and self-denial, the acceptance of suffering and responsibility, all these reflect the oblative, sacrificial love of the Redeemer and intensify the partners' life of grace. Their sexual life naturally belongs in this sacramental exchange of love.

Love is uniquely expressed and perfected through the marital act. The actions within marriage by which the couple are intimately and chastely united are noble and worthy ones. Expressed in a manner which is truly human, these actions signify

[13] Eph. 5. 24.
[14] 1 Cor. 7. 14.

and promote that mutual self-giving by which the spouses enrich each other with a joyful and thankful will.[15]

For the Christian sexuality has been assumed into the sphere
of the redemption. In the words of Teilhard de Chardin, passion
is placed at the service of Christ. Sex, then, promotes the community of charity in which husband and wife encounter Christ.
Theologians differ on the relation between sex and sacrament.[16]
They debate as to whether the marital act is a cause or an occasion
of grace, as to whether it is objectively (*ex opere operato*) or subjectively (*ex opere operantis*) sanctifying. On this Leonard Gerke
has a useful comment:

> That in the marriage sacrament the *opus operatum* and the
> *opus operantis* are so easily confused results from the very
> nature of this sacrament. In matrimony alone, among all the
> sacraments, the sacramental sign consists wholly in acts of the
> recipients of the sacrament; and what is more, these acts are,
> at least in their objective content or meaning, essentially ex-
> pressions of love or charity, and thus they will be placed all
> the more truly and rightly the more they are also subjectively
> filled with love or charity.[17]

The whole family unit lives in an atmosphere of grace, not in
virtue of any element added to it from outside, but in virtue of
the fact that it is a Christian family, a cell in the Body of Christ,
an *ecclesiola*, charged with the task of handing on the faith and
extending the community of charity. Its sanctifying force must
be enriched by prayer, sacramental practice and moral initiative,
but this force is essentially built into the fibre of family life. The
Christian works out his salvation in and through marriage, not
in spite of it, nor by opting out of it. The intertwining of secular
and sacred mission in Christian marriage gives it its particular

[15] Vatican II, Const. *Gaudium et Spes*, 49.
[16] See H. Doms, *The Meaning of Marriage* (London, 1939), ch. 10 (*Vom
Sinn und Zweck der Ehe*) (Breslau, 1935); E. Boissard, *op. cit.*, pp. 75–83;
H. Rondet, *Introduction à l'étude du mariage* (Paris, 1960), pp. 153–5;
C. Colombo, "Il matrimonio sacramento della nuova legge", in *La Scuola
Cattolica*, 91 (1963), p. 25; L. Gerke, *Christian Marriage, a Permanent
Sacrament* (Washington, 1965), pp. 72–90, 119–24, 146–50.
[17] *Op. cit.*, p. 147.

spirituality. As a secular reality it shares in mankind's responsibility for history and for the world; as a sacred reality it shares in the Church's responsibility for the redemption of all creatures. The Christian is called on to humanize and civilize the earth and to be a redeeming force, radiating the power of Christ in ever-widening circles over space and time. Their love preaches Christ: "By this shall all men know that you are my disciples, if you have love one for another."[18] This is an irresistible motive of credibility for the Christian faith. This is the true apologetic which makes men aware of the call within themselves, when they read their possibilities in the achievements of others.

Marriage consent takes all its meaning from the marriage relationship which it initiates. The marriage of Christian man and woman is their consecration to a mission, their dedication to the task of continuing the redemption through their life together as husband and wife and as father and mother. In marrying, the Christian commits himself formally as a Christian, he engages himself to actualize the potential of his baptism. If baptism is a pledge to follow Christ, to be with and for Christ, marriage is the application of this pledge to a concrete situation which has been blessed by Christ as a particular way of the Christian life. Baptism makes marriage a sacrament.[19]

The act of marrying is a high point in the person's experience. It is a moment of destiny. The symbolism of the ring, the acceptance of a single name, and the whole ceremony of the wedding underline the fundamental seriousness of his decision. In his *yes* he has mortgaged the future and has pledged to share his whole life with another. This is always a letting go, a leap into the unknown, an act of surrender. In an irreversible declaration of trust in himself and in this other he gathers all that he is and all that he has into a single act of giving.

The act of marrying is likewise a high point in the Christian life. It is a culminating moment, a moment when Christ draws near and addresses to the partners his typical invitation: "Come,

[18] John 13. 35.
[19] On the relationship between baptism and marriage see O. Casel "Die Taufe als Brautbad der Kirche", in *Jahrbuch für Liturgiewissenschaft*, 5 (1925), pp. 144–7. This was translated by J. Hild, "Le bain nuptial de l'Eglise", in *Dieu Vivant*, 4 (1945), pp. 43–50.

follow me." In this moment the partners solemnly accept a mission which is to polarize their whole lives. They surrender themselves not just to one another and to the future but to the providence of God and Christ's abiding promises. The blessing of the priest is the Church's endorsement of their decision. It recalls the wedding ceremony in the *Book of Tobias*:

> And taking the right hand of his daughter he (Raguel) gave it into the right hand of Tobias, saying: "The God of Abraham, and the God of Isaac, and the God of Jacob be with you. And may he join you together and fulfil his blessing in you."[20]

[20] Tobias 7. 15.

C. Jaime Snoek

Marriage and the Institutionalization of Sexual Relations

THERE is probably no other area of life in which the discrepancy between official morality and actual practice is as alarming as the field of our sexuality. In the teaching of the Churches, marriage is considered as the exclusive setting for sexual relations. All pre- or extra-marital sexual activity is seen as excluding from the Kingdom. Furthermore, it was not the Churches that invented this marvellous institution of marriage; it is the mature fruit of long human experience, and came into being initially merely to safeguard the continuance of the species through a guarantee of parental care and a certain minimum of economic stability. It has known greater and lesser degrees of flexibility in its history, with more or less pre- and extra-marital freedom.

In Judaism this flexibility gradually diminished through an evolution in the direction of strict monogamy, in which exclusive and faithful love was seen as a reflection and actualization of the Covenant itself. Confirmed and purified by Jesus, this vision has marked the whole of Western civilization. Despite numerous concessions on the part of society, concessions institutionalized in the form of prostitution, increased income when a child comes of age, desertion, divorce, or legal recognition of the position of the "companion" and her children, sexual relations are still officially confined to the married state. Until recently, social control was also strengthened by fear of pregnancy or venereal disease.

All this has changed very quickly. Antibiotics and contraceptives have taken the risk out of sex like a filter taking the poluting elements out of smoke. Demythologized and desacralized, sexuality no longer tolerates the slightest restrictions. The new generation rebels against the impositions of a hypocritical society: "make love, not war". Exposed to the constant bombardment of erotic stimuli with which our consumer society tries to seduce its customers, modern man questions the reasoning behind the prohibitions. Why should a sexual relationship have to be an expression of total and irrevocable commitment? What is immoral about a sexual relationship in the occasional and deliberately transitory amorous encounter? Why can sex not be experienced as a mere diversion? Why should sexuality be placed in a different context from other human relationships, as if it required a moral code other than that of mutual respect? Should it not be left to the partners themselves to decide what meaning or value they wish to attach to their sexual encounter? Why should all sexuality be confined to an institution designed to ensure procreation? Can life not offer anything richer than an institution? Does religious marriage still have any meaning? What has society at large to do with sexual behaviour which takes place between two people in secret? What right do the Churches have to say that certain sexual practices will exclude one from the Kingdom? Is this not just another example of the Church being behind the times, dragging itself in the wake of events, as usual?

And so one could go on. There is a new life-style, characterized by ample sexual freedom, imposing itself everywhere. Little remains of traditional morality beyond a façade. Virginity is taboo. Girls are claiming the same freedom that boys never gave up. Petting and pre- and extra-marital sexual relationships are the rule, at least in towns. The motor car has proved to have advantages which its inventor never envisaged. As a result of this "advancement" of women, prostitution, which served to protect the virginity of young ladies by providing an escape valve for male impetuosity, has lost most of its meaning. More telling than statistics of the Kinsey Report type is the celebrated report of the British Council of Churches. The thirteen theologians, who had assembled to prepare a declaration that would back up the traditional Christian moral view of sexual relations, in fact reached somewhat different conclusions.

So theology finds itself faced with a real challenge. It is no longer possible to try to evade the task of radically re-thinking the whole question.

I

A preliminary question is the legitimacy of questioning at all. Many will feel shocked by the simple fact of anyone today daring to cast doubt on the absolute and immutable nature of the traditional norms in this field. Having been conditioned for centuries by an authoritarian and monolithic process of indoctrination, man now seems to be challenging this on the level of the collective unconscious. The price he is now paying for his new self-discovery, which must be the will of God, is an initial shock and an increased feeling of insecurity. He now has to take on a creative role in the construction of his world, the elaboration of its customs and its laws. It was clearly much easier in the days when the Church, which knew everything, made the rules. Nevertheless, a decisive step has been taken in theological thinking and in the life of the Church in the last few years: it has become not only legitimate, but even necessary, to test all our ethical norms anew against the Gospel and against the only really absolute value—that of Love, to test them constantly to find out how much they contain of the true humanity that was revealed to us by Jesus Christ. In view of the importance of this new moral vision for the subject-matter of this article, it will be useful to examine it a little more closely.[1]

Basically, it is a question of the relationship between Covenant and Law, between Faith and Ethos. What comes to us from God, as a free gift of the Covenant, as grace, is love, the capacity to love, to take the existence of our brother on ourselves before God, as Jesus took the existence of all of us on himself. As a gift of the Covenant, this love can only be accepted in the freedom of faith, can only be celebrated in the action of grace. It is on this level that we decide formally between good and evil, between salvation and condemnation, because, in the final analysis, it is

---

[1] The idea developed here is based on the report on "the Christian's attitude to the world" produced by the Dutch Pastoral Council. Cf. *Pastoraal Concilie van der nederlandse kerkprovincie*, 4 (Amersfoort, Katholiek Archief, 1969), pp. 6–59.

a question of fidelity or infidelity to the Covenant with the Living God. But it falls to man, inspired by faith, and in the community of like-thinking men, to translate this basic ideal (which is both gift and task at the same time) into customs and norms, structures and institutions. These ethical norms then, to the extent that they represent the faithful expression of the ideal for a given historical situation, an expression worked out by the particular community that is living this historical moment of its culture, and to the extent that man in this situation sees in them, at least vaguely, the call of the Living God, constitute the Law of the Covenant. Infidelity to them will then be infidelity to the Living God himself, will be sin.

So the law is good. It teaches the way to grace. It translates the gospel ideal into concrete reality, allows it to be assimilated by the community and handed on to posterity. But it is also necessarily limited. What is valid in life on the existential plane can never be adequately expressed on the noetic plane. The law, in its historical formulation, is inevitably provisional in character. When it is made immutable, it can turn against man and against the Covenant, absolutizing what is relative.

So very fidelity to faith forces us constantly to re-think our ethical norms, particularly at times of great historical upheaval. This will be the task of a whole civilization, a whole people, the whole Church in dialogue with the world. Instinctive perception usually precedes reflective understanding and easily comes into conflict with a law that is still in force even though it no longer corresponds to the reality of the situation. In this process, with its inevitable and healthy tensions, the task of theology is the delicate one of helping the community "to test everything and hold on to what is good", to work out a new synthesis, to offer a stimulus towards the reformulation of the ideal with new validity.

II

The sexual ethic cannot be left out of this process. The main lines of the evolution of the sexual ethic in the ambit of Christianity and Western civilization are sufficiently well known today. Schillebeeckx has shown how this evolution has always aimed at safeguarding the basic value of human dignity.[2] This is also the heart of the question we are considering. So before moving on to the specific subject of this essay, let us try to assimilate some theses of the sexual ethic. I should like to put forward three propositions.[3]

1. Sexuality is a serious matter affecting the basic human situation, as an invitation offering the radical possibility of taking man outside himself, to live for another person, in the direction of liberation and self-realization, or, if he refuses the invitation, in the direction of self-enslavement, alienation and self-extermination.

This seriousness of sexuality should clearly not be seen as excluding the playful element inherent in all healthy eroticism, linked as this is to festivity, dancing, poetry and song (as in the Song of Songs), as a respite from the seriousness of work and society, just as religious celebration should also have a playful element proper to rest from work. But one has to get away from a purely recreational and infra-ethical view of sexuality, which, like any other form of diversion, also requires a more serious engagement in the sense of encounter with a "thou". Sexuality, in fact, has to do with life and death. Harvey Cox criticized the Playboy outlook not on the grounds that it was excessively sexual, but precisely because it was anti-sexual.[4] So true sexuality involves the whole person. To reduce it to mere genitality is a new form of dualism, more subtle (and no less dangerous) than the Manicheism from which we have hardly yet freed ourselves.

2. Sexuality is only fully human and moral when it is historically and culturally institutionalized.

It is an observable fact that sexuality is regulated in every culture. This is a requirement for the survival of society and of individuals. Examples of this are the law of exogamy and the prohibition of incest.[5] This universal fact stems from something that I take here as a basic fact—the radically social nature of human existence. The construction of laws, institutions and history is

[2] E. Schillebeeckx, "Changing Christian Concepts concerning Marriage", in *DO-C Dossier*, no. 224.
[3] These propositions are inspired by J. Ratzinger, "Zur theologie der Ehe", in *Theol. Quartalschr.*, 149 (1969), pp. 53–74.
[4] H. Cox, *The Secular City* (New York, 1965; London, 1966), p. 204.
[5] H. Schelsky, *Sociologie der Sexualität* (Hamburg, 1955), pp. 25–49.

natural to man; this is certainly true of the primordial form of human relationships represented by sexuality. The personalist view which, since Doms, has corrected the naturalist view of scholasticism, does not escape, for its part, from a certain unilateralism. It sees only the "I" and the "thou". And yet for sexuality to be fully human and salvific it is not enough for the "I" to be torn from his solitude by a "thou"; the two then have to have the courage to insert themselves into the history of their people, dedicating themselves to its future in acceptance of the fact that they will become its past. In the final analysis, this social dimension of sexuality contains a reference to the Absolute. And it is important to note that this appeal to the social, legal aspect is not a fortuitous element, but constitutive of sexuality itself.

It is clear that a multiplicity of cultures will lead to a multiplicity of customs and institutions designed to socialize and institutionalize sexuality. These will be valid to the extent that, within their cultural context, they serve to promote and actualize the ideal of humanity in general.

3. In the view of faith, the true community is that constituted by the initiative of God, bringing together men of all nations and all cultures. True history is the history of the People of God, whose origins are in the Creation and the Covenant, and whose definitive realization has been initiated in Jesus' Pasch. The indefectible fidelity of God who showed himself in the mystery of his Son is reflected concretely in the mystery of man and woman who, in their total and irrevocable gift of themselves, the fruit of grace, reproduce the love and fidelity of the God of the Covenant.

In this view the sexual duality ordered in the creation is already seen in the perspective of the Covenant, and eros in the perspective of *agape*. Matrimony is the privileged place for experiencing the love that saves. Like the Church itself, the marriage sacrament is an institution of faith itself; it forms part of the law of faith.

This institution, precisely because it is an institution of faith, is set apart in its essential structure from the autonomy of ethics. The good news of salvation through the marriage sacrament will, of course, be an important element in evangelization, particularly when this is directed to peoples with different cultures—

polygamous societies, for example. But it must be announced really as good news, if it is to be accepted in the freedom of faith, not imposed juridically. As the Gospel is assimilated, this good news will gradually transform customs, like a leaven. The proclamation of this message, and the living of it with simplicity and joy in the midst of the nations, is, together with religious celibacy, the most effective form of Christian presence in the bosom of humanity and the most useful form of *diakonia* that Christians can offer to humanity.

It remains to be seen whether the institutionalization of sexuality in the sacrament of marriage excludes any other sexual activity as being incompatible and immoral. This is what we must turn to now.

III

We can distinguish three different situations: first—unions that have a certain stability without reaching the fullness of the evangelical ideal; second—sexual relationships that can be called pre-marital in the strict sense of the word, that is, between engaged couples; third—sexual relationships with no compromise, the casual experience of love, the *amourette* or even "one night stand".

For the first, it would be possible, with some patristic foundation, to compile a whole range of relationships approximating by degrees to the true marriage of the sacrament, monogamous and indissoluble.[6] The second marriages of widows and widowers, for example, does not have the same fullness. In a different way there is something lacking in those cases of baptized persons, so numerous in some regions of Latin America, who simply "join together". There is also a certain incompleteness attaching to marriages between Christians and non-Christians. Further away still from the ideal would be remarriages of people whose ecclesiastically recognized marriage has irretrievably broken down. And then there are, in this changing world of ours, a number of other stable relationships whose protagonists would not think of them as marriages. Where does one draw the dividing line

[6] Cf. O. Rousseau, "Divorce and Remarriage: East and West", in *Concilium*, April 1967 (American edn., vol. 24).

between fidelity to the Gospel and betrayal of its ideal? The answer is not an easy one by any means, and will not be the same for all times and all places. On the question of divorce, for example, it is clear that Jesus refused to give a casuistical answer. And the Church since then has tried not to be unfaithful to his word, adopting an attitude of compassion in special cases. In the East, particular consideration is still given to the case of the abandoned "innocent" party. In the Latin Church there is evidence now of a growing desire to see greater respect accorded to personal decisions taken in all seriousness in these painful circumstances, and less discrimination against people who find themselves in these situations. But perhaps it would not be a good idea—it was Ratzinger who pointed this out—to institutionalize what Jesus refused to institutionalize: the law of faith is a single one—monogamous and indissoluble sacramental marriage.[7]

A similar problem, which has not been fully tackled, arises from the confrontation between the Church and polygamous cultures. Historically, this occurred for the first time in the sixteenth century, with the evangelization of the New World. The experience was not a happy one. The Church simply tried to import its canon law, which originated in a completely different type of culture; it quite failed to understand polygamous customs, let alone change them. They continue largely unaltered, albeit clandestinely, in the moral code of the *"casas grandes e senzalas"* (large households and slave quarters).[8]

With regard to the second situation (strictly pre-marital sexual relations), without wishing to deduce what should be done from what actually is done (which would be statistics ethics!), one has to admit that the rapid generalization of sexual relations between

---

[7] Ratzinger, *op. cit.*, p. 73.

[8] Cf. E. Hoornaert, "A Igreja Latina diante do Casamento", in *Rev. Ecl. Bras.*, 27 (1967), pp. 889–910. *Casa grande e senzala* is the title of a work by the prominent Brazilian sociologist, Gilberto Freyre. It is not easy to see any other solution to this problem, though perhaps one way might be a certain severing of the links between baptism and marriage. The Church would, as it were, not take cognizance of the polygamous situation of its neophytes, but would only solemnize, after a course of matrimonial catechesis, the marriages of those in a position to take the vows of exclusivity and indissolubility.

engaged couples makes one think. The more positive approach to sexuality which is general in our day, the greater degree of continuity seen between engagement and marriage, the varying ethical standards with their consequent varieties of behaviour models—all these factors are part explanations. Young people, it seems, no longer see any reason for the traditional ruling. Let us put the problem more specifically: it is generally accepted that any precipitation of genital contact marks and impoverishes the relationship, but, given the degree of maturity attained by those who are drawing near to the married state, should each and every form of sexual relationship be excluded as immoral? And if so, why?

The biblical precepts, at first glance, are not conclusive. St Paul, placed in the situation of having to reflect on what attitude the Christian should take to a pagan ethos, included *pornéia* among the works of the flesh which exclude one from the Kingdom. But recent authorities cast doubt on the absolute nature of this prohibition.[9] Furthermore, just what does St Paul mean by *pornéia*? (Incest? Prostitution? Sex without love?) And on whose authority does he condemn it—is it in virtue of a precept of the Lord's, or the apostolic interpretation of the gospel ethos for that time and place, or a personal interpretation? Without a precise reply to these questions, it is difficult to evaluate the exact import of Paul's pronouncement.

Another question: What would the early Church's attitude have been to those Christians who came over from Judaism? It would appear that Jews were allowed, at least in certain areas, to have sexual relations from the time of their "espousal".[10] It is then *a priori* highly unlikely that as Christians they would later have been obliged to renounce this custom.

If there is nothing precise in the biblical precepts, perhaps it is possible to base the traditional ruling on the overall revaluation of love and marriage found in the Bible, as confirmed by contemporary anthropology? This is what Böckle tries to do in an excellent study.[11] His approach can be summarized in the following

---

[9] Cf. H. Poehlmann and V. Schurr, "Vorehelicher Sexualverkehr?", in *Theol. Gegenw.*, 11 (1968), pp. 207–12.
[10] Cf. M.-J. Lagrange, *L'Evangile selon Saint Luc* (Paris, 1927), p. 26.
[11] F. Böckle and J. Köhne, *Geschlechtliche Beziehungen vor der Ehe*

syllogism: "The sex act as a total gift of love requires the guarantee of the marriage bond to attain its full meaning. Now the
Christian, in response to God's will, should always aim at attain-
ing the fullest meaning of love. Therefore his sexual relations
have to be confined to the married state." It is a trenchant conclusion: without the structure of marriage there can be no justification for sexual relations. In emergency situations there is a
plank to be grasped: the extraordinary form of Canon 1098.
But Böckle does make one very important qualification: the
norm is valid for a particular historical context, and neither
claims to be binding on other cultures nor excludes the possibility of a future evolution of our own.

Personally, I should be nothing like as categorical. The advantages of pre-nuptial continence can undoubtedly be great: a
happy expectation, a time of waiting full of promise, a future-
looking proof of love and fidelity; equally, the damage done by
anticipation can be considerable, due to the lack of a background
of living together to support the relationship. Yet it remains true
that continence alone will not necessarily assure the success of
the marriage, any more than previous experience will necessarily compromise it. Ell and Klomps posit the case of a young
man much tempted in other directions and ask moralists whether,
in such a case, sexual relations with his fiancée would not
strengthen the engagement, and so the subsequent marriage.[12]

I wonder whether it would not be possible to reconsider the
old concept of *"matrimonium in fieri"*. In a certain sense, marriage is always in a state of being made, though not in the strict
sense of the concept I am referring to. In the traditional concept
itself there are three distinct elements: the "Yes" of the partners,
the "Yes" of the Church, and the consummation. This process
could be interrupted after the first stage, and, with dispensation,
even after the second. In view of the greater continuity felt today
to exist between engagement and marriage, I should ask whether,
in some circumstances, it would not be permissible for the partners to place the consummation before the assent of the Church.

(Mainz, 1967). Cf. also J. Leclercq, *Mariage naturel et mariage chrétien*
(Tournai, 1965); J. Gruendel, *Fragen an den Moraltheologen* (Munich,
1969), pp. 63–74; P. Ricouer, "La sexualité", in *Esprit* (1960).
[12] E. Ell and H. Klomps, *Jugend vor der Ehe* (Limburg, 1967).

The idea is not new: Sanchez and Cajetan both thought like this, and, as we have seen, it was customary in certain spheres of Judaism at the time of Christ.

So far we have not moved away, strictly speaking, from traditional institutions. But the degree of sexual freedom supposed by our third situation, that of fleeting amorous encounters, no longer fits into the same framework. It seems as though a cosmic force, held back for centuries, has now burst the old dam, and is flooding everywhere like a tidal wave. Perhaps it is the historical destiny of man in the last part of this century to channel this force once more into service of the new man. A new era is certainly coming upon us, and is going to affect all our institutions, even marriage, the basic institution of our present civilization. Humanity is entering on a new and awesome adventure. It is as though we were setting foot for the first time on a new planet, not knowing what we are likely to meet. In the meantime we are clearly in the throes of an excessive reaction against the old ways. Malcolm Muggeridge talks sarcastically of a new right of man, the right to orgasm.[13] López Ibor speaks of the tedium brought about by the divorce of sex from *agape*, and warns against the clamour for "naturalness", which, he thinks, runs the risk of degenerating into something sub-natural or even inhuman.[14]

How will the man of tomorrow live his sexual life? Will he have won greater inner freedom? Will he have destroyed the tyranny of genitality and replaced it by a more discreet form of eroticism, more widespread, more communicative, permeating all human relationships? Will the differences between the sexes go on tending to diminish? Will marriage still be the basic structure of the civilization of tomorrow? Or are we heading for the "urban kibbutz" envisaged by one futurologist?[15] How will man face up to his responsibilities in the field of eugenics and population control?

There is no end to possible speculations and questions. Ethics

[13] Quoted in J. López Ibor, *El Libro de la Vida sexual* (Barcelona, 1968), p. 11.

[14] *Ibid.*, p. 27.

[15] S. Lemos, quoted in the *Jornal do Brasil*, 10 May 1968, "21st Century, Total Sex".

builds on facts and experiences, but its task goes beyond them. It has to show the direction that should be taken. As a tentative step in this direction, and by way of conclusion, let me put forward a few theses:

1. The mystery of the man-woman relationship must, ethically, remain beyond the limits of any developments in human engineering.

2. Monogamous and indissoluble marriage, as the best framework for the full human realization of total communication of love and the ideal matrix for the new human being, must remain the ideal institutional setting for sexual relations even in the civilization of the future.

3. The new patterns of sexual behaviour that are still to be worked out should be at the service of true, personalizing communication. Their validity will depend on the extent to which they contribute to the greater stability of marriage and the family.

4. Christianity is bound to make its contribution to the working out of the new ethos, in fidelity to the Gospel, which is basically concerned with the dignity of man. The Churches would do an extreme disservice to humanity if they were merely to let themselves be dragged along in the wake of the spirit of "the world".

What we are experiencing now—a frenzied propaganda for sexual freedoms—would seem to be rather a moment of antithesis in the dialectic of history and not a response. Let us try to test everything, to hold on to what is good. When, like the Lord, we propose guidelines or even rules for sexual conduct, let us do so as an announcement of the good news, like the law of the Covenant, which is grace and freedom rather than precept.

Translated by Paul Burns

Bernhard Häring

Pastoral Work among the Divorced and Invalidly Married

PASTORAL work in this connection should not be thought of in the narrow sense of restoring the affected parties to the sacraments. Primary is the practice of the life of faith and the anchoring of trust in God, and Christian love. It is not only a question of regularizing a marriage but also of helping the couple concerned to love one another in a way that brings them nearer to God. They can themselves become examples of a right attitude to marriage by humbly confessing their faults to their friends, and by urging others not to resort to divorce, or at least not to remarry should they do so. By bringing up their children well, they can be a good example to others. They can play their part in the apostolate. By resolutely refusing to discriminate, those engaged in pastoral work will encourage others in the Church community to behave similarly towards the couples concerned.

I make these initial comments in order to make it clear from the outset that nothing in this article should be taken as an attempt to restrict the scope of this type of pastoral work to mere sacramentalism. Naturally enough, believing that the Church is the sacrament of reconciliation whose centre is the Eucharist, the question of readmitting the partners of such marriages to the sacraments will not be ignored. One often hears it said that even when divorced couples who have remarried outside the Church are for ever excluded from the sacraments, they can for their comfort be reminded of these words of the Lord: "he who comes to me I will not cast out" (John 6. 37). But is that really good enough? Isn't it an unacceptable restriction of the Church's sacramentality? Through the Church, Christ wants to make his redemptive love sacramentally visible, in the spirit of Leo the Great's comment: *"Quod redemptoris nostri conspicuum fuit in sacramenta transivit"*.[1] The Church, surely, should be at least as visibly welcoming as Christ to sinners who do penance and sincerely seek God's will? And could such a welcome exclude the "visible signs of grace"?

I. PASTORAL QUESTIONS IN A NEW CONTEXT

Pastoral attitudes should respond to the needs of the time and to man's own awareness of himself. A standard that proved fruitful in one culture could be damaging in another. Consider, for example, the legal and pastoral discrimination against unmarried mothers and illegitimate children. Although this was never a typically Christian attitude, it could feature as one of the defences against pre-marital and extra-marital sex. But the same sort of attitude today would simply strengthen the massive trend towards the systematic use of contraceptives and abortion.

The situation is similar with regard to the permanent exclusion of invalidly married people from the sacraments. This is a measure that needs to be seen against the prevailing social background and its particular circumstances, for it was this social milieu, its economic and social structure, that guaranteed marital stability, and in which the separated partners were received back into their own families. In addition, there was a substantial group of unmarried people, peasants and unskilled workers, for whom marriage was made impossible by hopeless economic circumstances. All this was considered normal. Those who nevertheless married outside the Church knew themselves to be public sinners and so considered it proper that they should be excluded from the sacraments.

But nowadays the victims of broken marriages are in a much more painful position. They are legion and rootless. And as industrialization has made marriage possible for everyone, it is seen as one of the most important basic human rights. Alone and isolated, separated couples not only feel discriminated against, but frequently, and in spite of the best of intentions, fall victim

[1] Leo the Great, *Sermo* 72, *P.L.*, 54, 398.

to the grave temptations that arise from the worlds of work and leisure, and the widespread depersonalization of sex. Most of those whose marriages break up find it existentially impossible to grasp that for the sake of the Kingdom of Heaven they are expected to accept in courage and patience a future without marriage. They think it would be better to marry again than to endanger the marriages and moral lives of others.

In consequence of all this, and of contemporary ecumenism, the theology of marriage is also undergoing unrest. As the matter is hardly academic, the debate has to take place in public. The inadequacies of canon law's statements on marriage are widely discussed. And in addition there is the widespread growth of a critical attitude towards all structures that appear to confine or restrict life and happiness. It is in this atmosphere that people's consciences form and in which they subsequently make their conscientious decisions.

Often, even the most pious of pastoral workers is convinced that the partners to a marriage contracted outside the Church could not separate without doing themselves and their children real harm. When he sees the female partner of a broken marriage living in harmony with another man, and notes also that a firm relationship is developing between them, he is bound to heave a sigh of relief at this choice of a "lesser evil" when he recalls that this same woman had previously been driven to the verge of prostitution and promiscuity.

II. Towards Pastoral Solutions

I have no illusions with regard to unequivocal doctrinal solutions to these tricky problems. Our theological discussions of these questions must start from the standpoint of current Catholic teaching, though we must try to set in motion a reform of ecclesiastical legal thinking. Pastoral solutions should make every possible use of the possibilities that already exist.

In my opinion, well-intentioned Christians who are truly sorry for their sins and who have to the best of their ability maintained order in their lives, should not only be released from the bans of excommunication but should also be readmitted to the sacraments.[2] The readmission should be a demonstration of the truth that "God does not ask the impossible but through his commandments admonishes us to do what we are able to do, and for the rest, to pray".[3] This Augustinian principle, made more explicit by the Council of Trent, should be interpreted in context. Augustine is speaking of the man who welcomed the merciful Samaritan to his inn, and who, though already saved, still has much to learn.

The question of readmitting someone to communion poses more troublesome pastoral problems than readmission to the sacraments. In this connection ecclesiastical pluralism is necessary. There will be Eastern Christians brought up in an awareness of God's mercy who will simply not understand why people who are now living to the best of their ability and who have showed sorrow for past sins should be excluded from full participation in the Eucharist. Whereas in local communities of a more traditional stamp or of a more inbred cultural outlook such public forgiveness could give rise to scandal. In the case of public admission to communion, we are concerned with a process devolving upon episcopal authority, the facts of the case are known, and a fresh start is being made. But the situation is quite different when the partners of invalid marriages receive communion at times and places when and where their marital situation is unknown or where at least it is assumed that all is well. Those concerned should use their discretion. When there is public talk in the parish this can be a good opportunity for the parish priest to set the record straight in public.

But whatever the pastoral solution, we must be clear that both the theological discussion concerning the practice in the Eastern and Reformed Churches, and the search for merciful solutions in special cases, are doomed to failure unless the Church as a whole educates for fidelity through intelligent education for marriage, marriage guidance and constant reminders of the importance of forgiveness.

[2] Cf. J. G. Gerhartz, "Exkommuniziert—ein Leben lang?", in *Signum*, 41 (1969), pp. 44–50.
[3] Augustine, *De natura et gratia*, c. 43, 50, CSEL, 60, 270; cf. Denz.-Schön., *Ench. Symb.*, n. 1536–9.

III. The Different Personal Situations

The admission to the sacraments of divorced people who have not remarried presents no particular problems. But such people do need a lot of help if they are to make the best of their new position, and above all to find it in them to forgive and, if possible and desirable, achieve a reconciliation with a view to the resumption of married life.

For the invalidly married who continue to live together, re-admission to the sacraments should not be made quite so straight-forward. First, we should differentiate between the various possible situations:

1. In cases where it is canonically possible to regulate a union (for example, invalidly contracted mixed marriages, or remarriage after a first marriage that from the point of view of canon law was very probably invalid) there must be a desire to regulate matters in accordance with canon law. The tendency to minimize this aspect should not be encouraged. But if the legal process is made unreasonably difficult, or is unreasonably prolonged, then in my view it is not necessary to delay absolution until every legal hurdle has been overcome. The couple will often become convinced that in spite of outstanding legal complications they are, before God, properly married. Some couples, on the other hand, will feel themselves bound in conscience not to live as man and wife until the juridical aspects are settled once and for all. In every case there should be respect for conscience and a scrupulous avoidance of crude attempts to encourage an attitude or recommend a way of life that to this or that couple simply doesn't make sense.

2. In the many cases that cannot be resolved *in forum externum*, further important distinctions should be observed:

(*a*) It sometimes happens that those living a canonically invalid marriage are, for good reasons, convinced that their first marriage was not a proper one but they are unable to prove this conclusively in terms that will satisfy modern legal requirements. Significant in this connection are those cases in which a valid marriage was not consummated but dispensation was withheld on account of inadequate evidence. In so far as the subsequent marriage is a happy one, and the children well cared for, the couple will be firmly convinced that God has blessed their marriage. In these cases there should be no hesitation in giving sacramental absolution. If at the same time limitations are placed on the public reception of communion it should be made clear that this is not discrimination but merely the expression of necessary concern for the peace of the community and the avoidance of scandal.

(b) There may be other cases in which, subjectively, the partners are convinced that their second marriage is blessed by God, whereas the objective reasons supporting their claim that the first marriage was invalid are in some way inadequate or doubtful. Should one withhold absolution if in all other respects the disposition of the partners is good? I believe that there are certainly cases where the giving of absolution is indicated: for instance, when nothing good but quite possibly something harmful might result from an attempt to disturb their conviction.

Consider, for instance, those nominal Christians whom statistics ascribe to a Church or sect, who once contracted a marriage valid in the eyes of canon law but who then discovered it to be a grievous mismatch. Subsequently, and now happily remarried, they ask to join the Catholic Church. Should they be received in good faith, on condition that a return to their first partner is no longer possible?[4] It seems to me that the answer is "yes". I cannot see that this situation is much different from that of Catholics, once mere nominal Christians, who, now married a second time, now truly accept the faith. Provided the rightful demands of a third party for justice, or the good of the community as a whole, do not require it, it is my view that the couple's peace of conscience should not be disturbed and that absolution should not be made conditional upon the fulfilment of subjectively impossible conditions. Living together as "brother and sister" should only be required of a couple when this is anyway what their consciences recommend.

[4] This point becomes of yet greater importance if one hopes for the reunion of Christendom. Is it conceivable that when union comes the Catholic Church will subject to process of law all Orthodox and Reformed Christians who though happily married now have a broken marriage behind them and require them to prove either that the first marriage was invalid, or, if they cannot provide such proof, to separate?

3. Whereas in the case just mentioned the couple's *bona fides* testifies to their belief that their present marriage is a true one in the eyes of God, this is in some cases accompanied by the painful awareness that they should not have remarried and that their second marriage is not a true one, in spite of its exemplary nature. Nevertheless, they are genuinely convinced that out of responsibility for one another and their children they must live together. They look back on their past with deep sorrow and now try their best to live God's will as they understand it. Not infrequently, such people demonstrate their good faith by admitting their guilt in front of their friends and by advising others about to take a similar step to hold back.

The value of a partner's *bona fides* will depend on whether he is the guilty or the innocent party, and if guilty, whether or not he is conscious of and contrite about his part in the collapse of the first marriage. But guilty or innocent, a precondition is the conviction that a reconciliation cannot be achieved. The distinction between innocent and guilty party is of theological importance in the debate with the Orthodox Churches and their old tradition. Where it is a question of sacramentally proclaiming God's mercy and not of sanctioning a second marriage, the important consideration is an acceptable disposition, by which we understand sorrow for past sins and an earnest resolve to do God's will in the future. In cases where the collapse of a first marriage caused scandal, then extra care must be taken to avoid the giving of further scandal when determining the circumstances in which, now remarried, one or other of the former partners is admitted to communion among people who are aware of their earlier history.

IV. AN IMPORTANT DISTINCTION

To what extent does the pastoral practice I have recommended imply theologically that the Church can dissolve valid and consummated marriages and can authorize remarriage? I don't think it does. In other words, the pastoral solution suggested does not require any change in the Church's teaching. The Church is able to, and in my view should, bless a second but stable marriage rather than a doubtfully valid and hopelessly dead former marriage.[5] In this spirit, the way towards proper legal solutions seems to be open, at least for those who have justified doubts about the validity of their broken marriage. In this type of situation patronizing recommendations that do nothing for those concerned should be avoided. But the pastoral solutions I have suggested do not presuppose these legal reforms, desirable though they may be. I have not recommended that a priest be permitted to allow divorced people to remarry or that he should be able to declare a second marriage legally valid. Given the doctrinal and legal situation, both are unthinkable. My concern is for the credible proclamation of the divine mercy for contrite sinners who in a legally and ecclesiastically regrettable situation are prepared to do the best they can and who sincerely seek God's will. Where there is the honest conviction that doing their best includes ending their present relationship, or an attempt to live as brother and sister, then this is what must happen. But it would be unrealistic to maintain that this is possible or desirable in every case.

In what way is living together in this way, without sacramental recognition of their marriage, an aid to salvation? This is a theological question that can only be answered within the framework of the marriage debate as a whole. But from the purely pastoral viewpoint we can and must help those who live together in such unions to love one another with that respectful, patient and increasingly selfless love that will also give them a clearer idea of the love of God, and that will assist them to practise the Christian life as a whole.

[5] This inclination towards the *favor juris* was also suggested in the annexe on marriage put forward during the third session of Vatican II at the time when Schema 13 was being debated.

Translated by Mark Hollebone

PART II
BULLETIN

Gordon Dunstan

Development of the Theology
of Marriage in the Churches
of the Anglican Communion

IT IS hard indeed to speak of any "development" in pure theology in relation to marriage in the Anglican Churches today. There is widespread concern with institutional and practical questions concerning marriage—in particular the remarriage of the divorced and mixed marriages—and no doubt the theology of marriage is being probed in the attempt to find solutions to these questions; but of theological initiative there appears to be very little.

I

The last major theological contribution came from the work of Rev. Dr D. Sherwin Bailey, then assigned a research and teaching position on the staff of the Church of England Moral Welfare Council (a department of the National Assembly of the Established Church), and now Precentor of Wells Cathedral. His first, exploratory, study was *The Mystery of Love and Marriage*, significantly sub-titled "A Study in the Theology of Sexual Relation".[1] With insight, sensitivity and courage, Bailey explored the meaning of sexual love and of the union "in one flesh". The foundations of his theology of marriage were two: we may call them the myth in the Word, and the experience in the flesh. The myth he developed from the Genesis story, playing, in familiar fashion, on a literal construction of the Hebrew. The image of the triune God is to be sought in human beings in relation, in

[1] London, 1952.

133

the sexual bi-unity of man and woman together. As man "knows" himself only when he "knows" God, so a man "knows" himself when he "knows" his wife; carnal knowledge, in the lawyer's phrase, is the key to essential human knowledge, and the ground of the unity, the *henosis*, which is marriage. The book was avowedly exploratory; there were confusions inevitable in a pioneer work. But our theology of marriage, and of much else, still lives by the impetus which it gave.

In the midst of much teaching and occasional writing, Bailey developed his thought further in two major studies, *Homosexuality and the Western Christian Tradition*[2] and *The Man-Woman Relation in Christian Thought*.[3] In each the pattern was the same: an historical exploration, from the Bible, through the patristic and medieval periods, to the Anglican tradition; then a sketch of a theological interpretation bearing on the pressing problems of the day—problems of which he was actively aware as a pastor, and as a member of a small team of men and women engaged in formulating the contribution of the Church of England to the legislative processes of the English nation. Fundamentally, Bailey's position did not change: his final chapter was entitled "Towards a Theology of Sex", not of marriage: marriage is a product of the sexual relation, one institutional expression of it; marriage could not be understood except within the wider whole.

Bailey's position invited criticism, though it was widely accepted, developed and sometimes admiringly distorted in both England and the U.S.A. The present writer, though a disciple, friend and colleague of Bailey, criticized his two main foundations. In *The Marriage Covenant*,[4] I sought to ground marriage again in the consent, the purposeful commitment, of the spouses, retaining the sexual union as the consummation of that union, not its ground; I distinguished the covenantal view of marriage from a "low" contractual interpretation, and from a "high" doctrine, resting on the Genesis myth. Then, in an exposition of the notoriously difficult text, 1 Cor. 6. 16,[5] I denied that in biblical

[2] London, 1955.
[3] London, 1959.
[4] By G. R. Dunstan. London, 1961.
[5] "What? know ye not that he which is joined to an harlot is one body? for two, saith he, shall be one flesh."

usage the phrase "one flesh" carries the sexual overtones now imposed upon it. Rather, "it meant to the Jew very much what being 'one body' with Christ means to the Christian, namely, membership of a kinship group bound together by the strongest sense of mutual obligation" (see Judges 9. 2; 2 Sam. 5. 1). "It is more like the English common law concept of 'one person' to describe the man-wife solidarity."[6] This attempt, for what it is worth, to re-assert the primacy of *consensus* over *concubitus*, while in no way under-valuing the sexual endorsement in marriage, may be found, first, to allow for the potential completeness of the unmarried life more than the "one-flesh" school allows (which appeared to restrict the "image of God" to the married); and secondly, in its covenantal emphasis, to offer more ground for ecumenical accord, embracing Catholics, Orthodox, Anglicans, Protestants and the Reformed—an accord highly desirable as a preliminary to progress with the problems of mixed marriages.[7]

It was found to have its use, also, in the working out of a theology of marriage among African Christians keenly aware of —and, indeed, sensitive to—their own tribal traditions, anthropological and religious; whether (as was general) the marriage was arranged by the families concerned, or (as is becoming possible in a more mobile society) was a matter of choice between the parties, *consent* was of the essence of it—and this without any puritanical or dualistic under-valuation of the sexual life. Even the two stages of traditional Western medieval practice, the *sponsalia per verba de futuro* and the ratification and solemnization *per verba de presenti*, were recognized as a ground for combining some of the house-centred traditional African customs in marriage with the church-centred solemnities universal, in variant forms, in modern Christian practice.[8]

[6] G. R. Dunstan, "Hard Sayings—V", in *Theology*, LXVI (December 1963), p. 491.

[7] See, e.g., "Marriage and the Division among the Churches", in *Study Encounter*, III, 1 (1967), p. 2; a document used to initiate conversations between the W.C.C. and the Vatican, and so between the Vatican and some major non-Roman Churches. See also *Theology*, LXX (June 1967), pp. 241 ff., a special number devoted to mixed marriages.

[8] See *Report of the All-Africa Seminar on the Christian Home and Family Life; Rapport sur le Séminaire Panafricain sur le Foyer Chrétien et la Vie de Famille* (Geneva, 1963).

No doctrine of marriage, if it is to correspond to experience, will allow *consensus* and *concubitus* to be set at opposite poles, or to be isolated and exalted one against the other. Tendencies to do this have constantly to be corrected from the tradition. So G. W. Ashby, in a recent essay, has expounded Theodoret of Cyrrhus on marriage, emphasizing how he incorporated into the Greek patristic tradition the Old Testament and Hebraic understanding of the personal, the flesh-and-blood, and of God's creative act in the marriage of man and woman.[9]

II

Touching both the writing of pure theology and the wrestling with the institutional problems of marriage and divorce, stands the work of an Oxford philosopher, Helen Oppenheimer. In a recent article, entitled "Marriage and Grace",[10] Lady Oppenheimer considers marriage in the light of her earlier, more general, studies of immanence and the unity in plurality which is at the heart of Christian theology. In marriage—not specifically "Christian" marriage, but "the ordinary, human, secular phenomenon"—she finds an "immanence" which "can help to explain —or, on the other hand, can be illuminated by—our concept of God". Her earlier publications include two short but important books on Christian ethics and moral theology,[11] and in these, particularly in the first, *Law and Love*, she uses the model of "happy family life" (handling it with more than ordinary competence, precision and penetration) to illuminate the relation of the gospel precepts to a morality of laws, rights and duties.

> The Christian Gospel, if I understand it rightly, is the good news that what is natural but partial in our families can become universal, that through God's act human beings have been reinstated as God's children and can achieve the spirit of love through which they can transcend law. To treat Christianity as if it were itself a new law to be obeyed instead of a new system of personal relationships to be entered into is, as it were, to sidetrack the Holy Spirit.[12]

[9] G. W. Ashby, "Theodoret of Cyrrhus on Marriage", in *Theology*, LXXII (November 1969), p. 402.

[10] *Theology*, LXXII (December 1969), p. 535.

[11] Helen Oppenheimer, *Law and Love* (London, 1962) and *The Character of Christian Morality* (London, 1955).   [12] *Law and Love*, p. 30.

Elsewhere in the book the model is applied more widely, to deepen understanding of judgment, heaven and hell. Immediately, however, it is applied to the Church problem of divorce and remarriage. As, in the family, life is underpinned with rights and obligations but, when true to itself, rides above them, so in modern society divorce and remarriage remain a right conferred by the civil authority which the Christian, like any other citizen, may claim—but not *as a Christian*. The plain sayings of our Lord upon marriage and divorce are not to be minimized or interpreted away; they are to be taken as all of one piece with their context in the Sermon on the Mount, and so to be read, not as laws capable of juridical trial and enforcement, but as qualities which *will appear* in authentic Christian living; and so essential are they to Christian living that to ignore or defy them cannot be described as *Christian* acts, cannot be expected of a faithfully *Christian* Church.

> Whatever interpretation we give to Christ's teaching on divorce must also be capable of covering his teaching on anger, lust and going to law.

Therefore,

> while not judging other people, the Christian will always tend to reject remarriage after divorce for himself.

> The man who has remarried after divorce is like a man who has successfully sued his enemy for damages. The one has not necessarily been lustful in the ordinary sense any more than the other has necessarily been vindictive, but neither has acted in the Christian spirit.

The practice of the Church of England in admitting such remarried persons to the Holy Communion—preferring admission as a means of grace to exclusion as a penal instrument—is, accordingly, defended; but remarriage or a service of blessing in church is excluded:

> It is not legalism to say that the Church can hardly give its formal blessing to people when they are actually doing what Christ particularly wished them not to do.

In return,

> the Church should recognize, fully and not grudgingly, the validity

of a civil marriage after a civil divorce, just as it recognizes the validity of a civil lawsuit to redress a wrong.

Legally speaking (and at once the discussion passes outside the realm of *Christian* discourse), it is possible to be absolved from vows, even to God, and people can be released from marriages, so far as their legal and moral status is concerned.

> Whether or not they have broken their faith with God is for God only to judge; but to refuse them Communion is to deny the ordinary means for sinners to approach God and restore broken faith.[13]

Canon Hugh Montefiore, in a recent pamphlet,[14] argues to different conclusions. He is certain that Jesus did not legislate, but he falls far short of Lady Oppenheimer in the sense of the obligation that, in a Christian community, the words of Christ should be fulfilled. His argument is largely empirical, and to choose one epigram is not to sample it unfairly:

> If it is better to marry than to burn, it is better to remarry than to burn.

Therefore he would suggest that, in suitable cases,

> remarriage be permitted in England's parish churches, using the same service as we have now, with a prayer added admitting failure in the past, praying for forgiveness, and asking for future blessing.[15]

Both writers, Lady Oppenheimer and Canon Montefiore, serve on a Commission appointed by the Archbishop of Canterbury to report on the Christian doctrine of marriage, with obvious, though implicit, reference to the further problems of divorce and remarriage. The Church of England has lived for four hundred years with this problem and it is unlikely that this Commission will solve it. At the Reformation it inherited from the medieval Western Church the strictest possible doctrine of the indissolubility of a marriage validly celebrated between two baptized Christians and consummated; it also denied itself the benefit of most of that elaborate system of safety-valves, the practice of nullification based on wide-ranging degrees of kindred and spiritual

---

[13] *Ibid.*, pp. 72, 74, 76–8.
[14] *Remarriage and Mixed Marriage: A Plea for Dual Reform* (London, 1967). (Canon Montefiore is now Bishop Designate of Kingston upon Thames.)
[15] *Op. cit.*, pp. 13, 17.

affinity within which marriage was forbidden, which had been used to mitigate the rigour of that doctrine in practice. Consequently its canon law forbade *divortium a vinculo*; the most its canon law has ever permitted was separation *a thoro et mensa*, with a caution against remarriage during the lifetime of the separated spouse; and since 1969, after two decades of experiment, the reading of a private service in church after civil marriage before the registrar.[16]

At the Reformation the ecclesiastical jurisdiction had been merged with the other courts of law under the supreme headship of the Sovereign, though the jurisdiction itself remained distinct, with its own procedures and practitioners. Jurisdiction over marriage remained part of the ecclesiastical jurisdiction until 1857; until that year divorce, in the modern sense, with liberty to remarry, was theoretically forbidden throughout England and Wales. In fact, there was an escape route for the very wealthy, by means of a series of legal actions culminating in a private Act of Parliament which in effect dispensed the petitioner from the prohibition of remarriage after a decree of separation in the ecclesiastical court; there were 317 such Acts passed between 1697 and 1855. Then by the first Matrimonial Causes Act, 1857, matrimonial jurisdiction was transferred from the ecclesiastical court to a new division of the High Court, and divorce with liberty to remarry became permissible, on grounds which have widened steadily as the internal logic of divorce took over from the logic of total prohibition. The ground of divorce was the matrimonial offence, taken over from the old ecclesiastical law; but even this, at the time of writing, will almost certainly soon be abolished, and the breakdown of marriage substituted for it.

So much for the law: an early total prohibition of divorce, soon mitigated by a dispensing power assumed by the High Court of Parliament; then an extending permission of divorce, steadily accepted throughout all ranks of society as social and economic changes (including legal aid—financial help from the State) made it possible for even the poorest to act upon it. Theology, however, did not always go along with law. From the very

[16] *Constitutions and Canons Ecclesiastical, 1604*, ed. J. V. Bullard (London, 1934), c. CVII. *The Canons of the Church of England* (London, 1969), cc. B 30–36.

beginning of the Reformation of England there have flowed two theological traditions, both of which are still represented in Anglican thought today. While the canon law, and the practice of the courts, still forbade divorce *a vinculo* there were theologians who would have permitted, theologically, remarriage after divorce on the ground of the Matthaean exception, and some on the ground of desertion as well, had the law allowed it. On the other hand there were theologians who retained an indissolubilist view, both then and since, and throughout the last century when divorce had become a civil liberty widely accepted.

Both traditions co-existed and co-exist. Their history has been traced by Rev. Dr A. R. Winnett in *Divorce and Remarriage in Anglicanism*.[17] The rising number of divorces which began with the beginning of the twentieth century, coming at a time of quickened self-consciousness in the Church as a body set against the State, and creating widespread alarm for the institution of marriage itself, won over much support for the indissolubilist view; so much so that by means of Resolutions in the Convocations of Canterbury and York, and in successive Lambeth Conferences, the indissolubilist view had become, by mid-century, the "official" view of the Church of England in particular, and of the Anglican Communion in general, leaving clergymen who exercised their undoubted legal right to solemnize the marriage of divorced persons with a sense of having offended morally against the mind and express judgment of the Church. Dr Winnett, in the final chapter of his book, abandoned the position of academic detachment held in its earlier chapters, and embraced the indissolubilist cause—though without convincing argument why he should have chosen that side rather than the other.

This position is now again under widespread and searching questioning. Dr Winnett has himself repudiated it in a new book, *The Church and Divorce: A Factual Survey*.[18] The main part of the book is indeed a factual survey of developments in the decade since his first book was published, developments in theology, Anglican, Roman Catholic and other, and developments in

[17] London, 1958.
[18] London, 1968. It was reviewed, with current Roman Catholic literature, by the present writer in an editorial article in *Theology*, LXXI (September 1968), p. 385.

practice, particularly in provinces of the Anglican Communion outside of England. The book is documented with the Resolutions of successive Lambeth Conferences and Convocations. It contains also comprehensive extracts from Canon XXVII, 1967, of the Canadian Church which, *inter alia*, defines conditions under which divorced persons may be remarried in church during the lifetime of the former spouse, and procedures to be followed to this end. A Commission, to be set up under the Canon, has to be satisfied that nine conditions have been met before it may authorize the marriage in church; the last of them is that

> The applicants understand the Christian Doctrine of Marriage as defined in this Canon, and intend to enter into such a marriage, and believe on reasonable grounds that they have the capacity to enter into and sustain the marriage during their joint lives.[19]

The emphasis on intention will be noted, with the presumption that this right intention is not frustrated *ab initio* by any *ligamen* from the past. The definition of marriage, referred to in this condition, is made in an extended Preface to the Canon, which also contains "built-in" provision for this particular exercise of the ecclesiastical jurisdiction:

1. The Anglican Church of Canada affirms, according to our Lord's teaching as found in Holy Scripture and expressed in the Form of Solemnization of Matrimony in the Book of Common Prayer, that marriage is a lifelong union in faithful love, for better or for worse, to the exclusion of all others on either side. This union is established by God's grace when two duly qualified persons enter into a contract of marriage in which they declare their intention of fulfilling its purposes and exchange vows to be faithful to one another until they are separated by death. The purposes of marriage are mutual fellowship, support and comfort, the procreation (if it may be) and nurture of children, and the creation of a relationship in which sexuality may serve personal fulfilment in a community of faithful love. This contract is made in the sight of God and in the presence of witnesses and of an authorized minister.

3. The Church throughout her history has recognized that not all marriages in human society conform, or are intended to conform, to the standard here described. For this reason, in the

[19] Quoted in Winnett, *op. cit.*, p. 52.

exercise of pastoral care as evidenced in the earliest documents of the New Testament, the Church has from the beginning made regulations for the support of family life especially among her own members.

4. Aspects of the regulation of marriage in the apostolic Church are recorded in the New Testament. . . . In Christ's name separated spouses were encouraged to seek reconciliation (1 Cor. 7. 10 f.). In his name also divorce was forbidden though not without exception (Matt. 5. 31 f.; Mark 10. 2–9; cf. Mal. 2. 13–16). In certain circumstances a believer already married to an unbeliever might be declared free from such a marriage bond (1 Cor. 7. 12–16); in others, and here in the name of Christ, remarriage during the lifetime of a former spouse was described, with one exception, as an adulterous union (Matt. 19. 9; Mark 10. 11 f.; Luke 16. 18; cf. Rom. 7. 3).

5. From these principles and precedents the Church . . . has sought in her rites and Canons to uphold and maintain the Christian standard of marriage in the societies in which believers dwell. This standard and these rites and Canons pertain to . . . the reconciliation of alienated spouses, and to the dissolution of marriage and its consequences.[20]

This model is undoubtedly being studied in other parts of the Anglican Communion, notably in Australia and in England. Even an unofficial, though powerful, body like the Mothers' Union, whose interpretation of its stated aim "to uphold the sanctity of marriage" is in fact expressed by excluding from membership, not only unmarried mothers, but also any woman who has been a party to divorce proceedings, whether as petitioner or respondent, is now deeply divided about its policy; its New Zealand branch has already departed from it, and in England it has set up a committee, chaired by the Suffragan Bishop of Willesden, to advise on the question.

The Church of England is in a position of peculiar difficulty. It has not only the double tradition among its theologians, to which reference has been made; it has not only a civil law which leaves to the parish priest a discretion whether or not to marry divorced persons in his church, and a policy, formulated by the

---

[20] *Canon XXVII: On Marriage in the Church*; enacted by the Twenty-third session of the General Synod of the Anglican Church of Canada, Ottawa, Ontario, 22 August to 31 August 1967, p. 1.

Convocations and supported by the bishops, requiring him to exercise that discretion negatively; it has also committed itself to the reform of the *secular* law of divorce, and to replacing the matrimonial offence by "the breakdown of marriage". It has come into this position through the work of a Group appointed by the Archbishop of Canterbury, and chaired by the distinguished moral theologian, Dr R. C. Mortimer, Bishop of Exeter.[21] The terms of reference given to the Group recognized "that there is a difference in the attitudes of the Church and State towards the further marriage of a divorced person whose former partner is living"; this distinction was emphasized *passim* in the Report, and particularly in a whole chapter devoted to "The Church's Concern with Secular Matrimonial Law"; and the Archbishop of Canterbury in a Preface to the published Report, wrote:

> If there were to be legislation on the lines of what is suggested in this Report, I believe that the Churches would still maintain their own pastoral discipline.

Nevertheless, many commentators have argued that the Church of England cannot consistently favour dissolution on the ground of "breakdown" by the civil power while purporting to maintain for itself a discipline which assumes the creation and permanence of a *vinculum matrimoni* made by the valid exchange of consent by competent parties—and consummated—whether that exchange be made in church before the priest and congregation or in the office of the civil registrar. The Archbishop's new Commission on the Christian Doctrine of Marriage has an unenviable task before it, and no one can yet predict the direction in which its thinking will move. There is one consolation: contraception came off the agenda with the Lambeth Conference of 1958, a decision which was only the more strongly confirmed when challenged by the publication of *Humanae Vitae* ten years afterwards.[22]

[21] See *Putting Asunder: A Divorce Law for Contemporary Society*. The Report of a Group appointed by the Archbishop of Canterbury in January 1964. (London, 1966.)

[22] See *The Family in Contemporary Society*: The Report of a Group convened at the behest of the Archbishop of Canterbury. (London, 1958.) *The Lambeth Conference 1958, Resolutions and Reports* (London, 1958), esp. Resolution 115. *The Lambeth Conference 1968*: Resolutions and Reports (London, 1968), esp. Resolution 22.

Heinrich Baltensweiler

Current Developments in the Theology of Marriage in the Reformed Churches

PROTESTANT teaching on marriage has undergone such great changes in the two decades since the last war that one can almost speak of a new image of marriage. In an essay entitled "The new Image of Marriage in Protestant Theology", Wenzel Lohff writes that "to summarize in one sentence the new image of marriage from the Protestant point of view, one could say that whereas traditional teaching regarded marriage in terms of the law and the order of things, the new image consists in understanding it in terms of the Gospel, as the benevolent gift of an authentic life realized in faith, which has the greatest power to elevate mankind" (*Dae neue Bild der Ehe*, ed., H. Harsch, Munich, 1969, p. 36).

This process of change did not, of course, happen overnight; it is to be seen far more as a development of thought which began after the Second World War and is still continuing today. The extensive literature on the subject (for details see: H. Baltensweiler, *Die Ehe im Neuen Testament*, Zürich, 1967, pp. 267 ff.; *Christliche Ehe und getrennte Kirchen* [documents, studies and international bibliography], ed. H. Stirnimann, Freiburg, 1968, pp. 95 ff.; D. W. Shaner, *A Christian View of Divorce according to the Teachings of the New Testament*, Leiden, 1969, pp. 110 ff.) is such that I shall examine only the main positions; restrictions of space do not allow of a complete survey; my aim here is thus to pick out a few salient points to exemplify the problem in question. I shall start by considering the causes of the present change in the image of marriage, and then attempt to sketch the gradual development of the new image, proceeding finally to the problem of divorce and remarriage as it presents itself in the Protestant Churches today.

The basic change in the doctrine of marriage can only be understood in the context of changes in the exegetical viewpoint since the last war. It is not a question of *new* sources being opened up; the old biblical statements on marriage, in particular those of the New Testament, still stand. But a consensus of opinion in Protestant circles has recently held that *direct* recourse to biblical statements is not possible. The Old and the New Testaments may well contain emphatic statements on marriage and divorce, but the concrete way in which marriage is actually lived involves a variety of spheres of human existence. Marriage belongs to the areas of religion, law, society and culture, which in their turn are all subject to change, be it environmental or dictated by time. Precisely because marriage can only be realized on a practical rather than on a theoretical level, it cannot avoid being affected by the changing circumstances of time. Even within the context of biblical testimony we find a development of the concept of marriage, in that a definite tendency to monogamy becomes evident (H. Ringeling, *Theology und Sexualität. Das private Verhalten als Thema der Sozialethik*, Gütersloh, 1968, pp. 225 ff.). Of course, there is a grave danger of imposing our own understanding of marriage on the New Testament texts; this must be avoided at all costs. It is not simply a matter of combining all relevant biblical texts to form a doctrine of marriage; instead, we should ask ourselves what these statements would have meant to contemporary listeners. The New Testament statements on marriage and divorce must be brought up to date, not merely repeated. What is needed is not a straightforward rendering of these declarations, but their interpretation in the light of the world today.

Protestant research in this respect acknowledges that nowhere in the New Testament is there a full teaching on marriage (H. Greeven, "Ehe nach dem Neuen Testament", in *New Testament Studies*, Vol. 15, 4, 1969, p. 365). This means that we are not justified in systematically co-ordinating the relevant statements; instead, each statement on marriage must be considered on its own merits and examined in its historical context. Hence we know today that Paul's declarations in 1 Corinthians are not to be understood as a definite doctrine of marriage, but as answers to particular questions put to him by members of the Church in Corinth. If we bear in mind that biblical testimony is rooted in a specific period of history, and that New Testament statements can be properly understood only within the context of contemporary attitudes, we shall appreciate the complexity of the issue. But another difficulty arises at this point: in the greater part of the New Testament, and in particular in the Epistles of Paul, ethical statements have to be seen in the light of hope in the world to come. It is obvious that a totally different judgment would be offered on marriage at a time when the Kingdom of God had been proclaimed and was expected at any moment than would be the case if this world was expected to persist. I do not feel that there can be any justification for simply applying to present circumstances certain declarations made by Paul in direct expectation of the Parousia, without any thought that he might have spoken very differently had he been confronted with the longer duration of the Church in this world.

It was usual in Protestant ethics before and directly after the Second World War to see marriage as part of the order of creation (cf. P. Althaus, *Grundriss der Ethik*, Gütersloh, 1953, p. 115; also K. Heim, *Die Christliche Ethik*, Tübingen, 1955, pp. 172 ff.). This notion was derived from the more static ideal of marriage which had moulded its structure in human life over the centuries. The true meaning of marriage might be obscured by sin, or neglected, but it could not be destroyed. In this way, E. Brunner could declare in *Das Gebot und die Ordnung* (Zürich, 1939) that marriage was a state which, though latent in man's natural consciousness, could not be naturally acknowledged; only through faith could we understand it as part of the order of creation. A closer scrutiny of Brunner's argument reveals that his train of thought stems from what is morally directly obvious. The concept of the order of creation in fact conceals a modern understanding of marriage, so one might as well dispense with the concept entirely. Should this not seem desirable, then the notion of marriage as part of the order of creation could at most be permissible in this form: "The present responsible attitude to faith sees this image of marriage as accordant with a belief in creation, but not in the sense that it is a simultaneously unhistorical yet universal basic structure of human existence" (cf. W. Lohff, *op. cit.*, p. 23). Accordingly, Protestant thought no longer allows of a static definition of the nature of marriage. This applies as well to the interpretation of Ephesians 5. 21–32, which Protestant exegesis would understand not as a description of the essence of marriage in the ontological sense, but as a representation in the functional sense of marriage actually being lived (cf. E. Käsemann, "Das Interpretationsproblem des Epheserbriefes", in *Exegetische Versuche und Besinnungen*, II, Göttingen, 1964, pp. 253 ff.).

In Ephesians 5 marriage is bound up with the Christ-event, thus revealing its true essence as something intended even at the Creation. The word of God on the union of man and woman as ordained by creation (Gen. 1. 2, 24) is seen as a prophetic allusion to the union of Christ and the Church, which enjoys the dimension of salvation history. It is clear that the above-mentioned passage in Genesis refers essentially to marriage, that is, to man and woman. If it is then applied to Christ and the Church, it not only has allegorical overtones but ultimately returns from its applied to its original sense—the relationship between man and woman. This relationship is foreshadowed in Christ and his relationship to the Church, as a new relationship basically intended in the Creation.

Hence the pattern of "prototype" and "copy" as used mainly by Protestant exegetes to elicit the real meaning of Ephesians 5 is inadequate; it would be more appropriate to use the term "representation" or "realization". In the same way that the Church as such represents Christ in this world, Christian marriage realizes the presence of Christ among us (cf. H. Baltensweiler, *op. cit.*, pp. 233 ff.). Marriage can thus be a true means of salvation, which can even be transmitted from the believing to the unbelieving partner (1 Cor. 7. 14).

Christian marriage is therefore not to be understood as merely an additional element to ordinary marriage; the latter is not intensified by Christianity. There is only one form of Christian marriage, which, while being lived like any ordinary marriage, allows the couple, by virtue of their Christianity, to view their marriage as something new. Christ is present not only in the Church, but in marriage, and thus transforms it into a means of salvation.

No daunting ideal is set before us; the promise of redemption and unity, founded in Christ, transcends the ordinary imperfect earthly marriage, which is thus freed from all natural considerations and conceived anew by God.

Paul, especially, regarded marriage (1 Cor. 7) in terms of divine vocation. Since he believed that the end of the world was close, he thought it better to lead a celibate life. This higher estimate of celibacy was not motivated by any aversion to the flesh, but seemed to offer men a greater possibility of serving God. Married and celibate in the final analysis are serving God, but whereas the latter achieve this as it were directly, the former accomplish it only indirectly through the things of this world. They aim at satisfying their partner, as is fitting, since marriage was divinely instituted; yet Christians should on no account overestimate marriage.

This is the meaning of the often misapplied words of 1 Corinthians 7. 29–31. It should be remembered that they can be understood only in the light of the contemporary expectation of the imminent end of the world, and that to read into them any command or invitation to spiritual celibacy would be grossly mistaken. It would in fact be totally impossible, since in 1 Corinthians 7. 3 Paul has spoken emphatically of the regular fulfilment of marital rights. He is not suggesting that Christians should be indifferent to the things of the world, including marriage, or that they should forcibly control their emotions; on the contrary, the Christian is expected to participate as full-heartedly in the sorrows of the world as in the happiness of those close to him. Marriage demands the total engagement of those concerned. There is no room here for any pretence. Paul makes this quite clear when, in verse 30, he says that one should buy as though one had no goods. The interplay of "buying" and "keeping" is symptomatic; one should not buy with any feeling of guilt or in the knowledge that it is basically wrong: what really matters is that the buying itself is not the most important issue. Paul is not in fact condemning buying as such, but rather a desperate clinging to possessions. With reference to marriage, this means that it should not *be* the ultimate, but a means to achieve it; in other words, it belongs to this world, and is thus transitory. Here Paul is wholly in accordance with the gospels, which similarly decline to accord marriage any ultimate significance: "For when they rise from the dead they neither marry nor are given in marriage, but are like the angels in heaven" (Mk. 12. 25 par.). This statement finally confirms the impossibility of marriage ever acquiring a glorified status within Christianity. The structure of marriage is temporal, transitory and bound only to this world. But precisely for Christians, it represents the means of serving and glorifying God in this world.

Consequently, the definite practice of divorce in the Israel of the Old Testament can be seen in a very different light. Christ condemned divorce on the grounds that the possibility of divorce had been permitted by God only on account of the hardness of men's hearts. But this had not always been so (Mk. 10. 5). For Christ, marriage was by its very nature indissoluble. Divorce resulted only from the hardness of the human heart blinding men to the final aim set by God. If marriage derives its true significance from Christ, then it is clear that the forgiveness bestowed by Christ on his Church should also be a part of marriage. For Christ, there are no grounds to justify the breaking up of a marriage. Any man who leaves his wife and marries another commits adultery (Lk. 16. 18). Even the so-called divorce clauses in Matthew (5. 32 and 19. 9) admit no justification for any departure from this ruling, since they are obviously additions determined by contemporary considerations. I have attempted to determine the relevance of these clauses to the life of the times, in connection with Bonsirven's thesis that they indicate a reference to irregular marriages. I have suggested that they refer to the marriages of proselytes, who, under Jewish law, had been able to marry within the forbidden degrees of affinity, and who subsequently became Christians. In Matthew's Church, such marriages had to be dissolved. Quite apart from whether this specific interpretation is eventually accepted (e.g., P. Bonnard in his commentary, *L'évangile selon Saint Matthieu*, Neuchâtel, 1963, pp. 69 and 283), there are increasing signs that the historical interpretation of the relevant passages in Matthew is beginning to hold within the Protestant Churches (see also H. Greeven, *op. cit.*, p. 382).

Jesus' insistence on the indissolubility of marriage is not to be understood as a binding declaration about marriage itself, in the sense that he actually said that marriage *could* not be dissolved. This demand must be understood in the context of all the demands made in the Sermon on the Mount, or indeed of any other ethical demands Jesus made. He did not preach a new law of marriage, but aimed rather at moving the hearts of men by his demands. He did not ask after what was permissible or possible, but sought the recognizable will of God within the law. His insistence on the indissolubility of marriage was aimed precisely at emphasizing the magnitude and beauty of the institution as intended by God.

The Protestant Churches are unanimously agreed that the legal prohibition of divorce would not correspond to the intention of Christ's words (H. v. Oyen, *Evangelische Ethik*, II, Basle, pp. 273 ff.; N. H. Søe, *Christliche Ethik*, Munich, 1957, pp. 302 ff.; R. Kaptein, *Ehescheidung und Wiederverheiratung*, Göttingen, 1963; H. Thielicke, *Theologische Ethik*, III, Tübingen, 1964, pp. 697 ff.; D. W. Shaner, *A Christian View of Divorce*, Leiden, 1969).

The Christian Church must emphasize and affirm the indissolubility of marriage as the essential intention, even if in certain concrete cases a divorce has to be permitted. We would then be making a decision along the lines set out by Paul in 1 Corinthians 7. 10–11. He accepts Christ's teaching fully and without limitation, but recognizes the facticity of divorce in a concrete instance. 1 Corinthians 7. 11 must obviously be understood in the sense that a woman (or a man), who is already divorced, can be accepted into the Church community, on condition that she (or he) remain unmarried or remarry the former partner. In other words, even if he permits divorce in actuality, Paul insists unequivocally on the will of God (G. Bornkamm, "Ehescheidung und Wiederverheiratung im Neuen Testament", in *Geschichte und Glaube* [Part I], III, Munich, 1968, p. 58).

Paul, therefore, in contrast to the words of Christ, allows for the possibility of and justification for divorce. This would seem to indicate that the Church today should in certain cases and situations make similar decisions. It is therefore a logical consequence of Pauline thought to continue this process, and to allow divorced persons a second marriage (cf. H. Thielicke, *op. cit.*, pp. 713 ff.; R. Kaptein, *op. cit.*). For if a *divorce* is really recognized as such, and not as a mere *separation* with the possibility of reconciliation (cf. W. Trillhaas, *Ethik*, Berlin, 1965, p. 291), then the divorced partners must be allowed to remarry. The danger should, however, be borne in mind that if such a position were to be taken by the Church, it could be seen as a concession, or as a relaxation of the original will of God, and thus a lax conception of marriage and divorce. It is therefore essential that the Church should always bear witness to the true creative will of God and help to effect a second marriage "only if sincerely, without concealing any existing guilt, it can ask forgiveness for and invoke God's blessing on those concerned" (G. Bornkamm, *op. cit.*, p. 59). Protestant opinion does not hold that the legal proscription of a second marriage after divorce could be of any more help to anyone than the legalistic interpretation of the requirement that marriage remain indissoluble.

Translated by Lucinde Tieck

PART III
DOCUMENTATION
CONCILIUM

Concilium General Secretariat

The Humanization
of Sexuality

FROM the viewpoint of theology,[1] there are at least two constant
tendencies in the recent profusion of writings about sexuality:
looking on sex as a new field for a variety of religious experience
—a neo-sacralization of sexuality;[2] and seeing the liberating element, now so heavily stressed in sexuality, as contributing to the
great revolution that would offer man new human awareness in
all aspects of social and cultural life.[3]

These two tendencies develop for the most part not only outside the Churches, but also outside established society. Most
theological writers on the subject are interested in the second
tendency, probably because the new anthropology, so strongly emphasized therein, asks Christians how this sexual revolution contributes to the liberation of man,[4] and also because it contains
elements of a critique of society which implies a critique of the

---

[1] G. Hummel, "Sexualität, Sexualethik, Sexualpädagogik", in *Luth.
Monatshefte*, 9 (Sept. 1969), pp. 417–23; D. H. Salman, "Bulletin", in
Rev. des Sc. Phil. et Théol., 53, 2 (April 1969), pp. 269–74).

[2] G. R. Scott, *Phallic Worship* (London, 1966); A. M. Greeley, "There's
a New Time Religion on Campus", in *The New York Times Magazine*
(1 June 1969), sect. 6, 17; *id., A Future to Hope In* (New York, 1969),
pp. 29–65: "Sex to love with".

[3] R. Reiche, *Sexualität und Klassenkampf* (Frankfurt, 1969); W. Reich,
Die Sexuelle Revolution (Frankfurt, 1966); J. van Ussel, "Het christendom
en de seksuele problematiek", in *Kultuurleven*, 35, 9 (Nov. 1968), pp. 658–
69.

[4] The Christian Churches are often accused of being solely responsible
for social alienation, which is the object of much modern protest. Van
Ussel (*op. cit.*, note 49) has pointed out that this alienation was created

Church.[5] This documentation is therefore mainly concerned with this second tendency.

What is happening in the sphere of sex is seen as part of a revolutionary attempt to create, in successive stages, a new human awareness in every sector of social life.

This revolution has certainly already been achieved to a great extent at the level of property and authority, and has been aided by the separation of wages from work, and by the transfer of authority from the institution and social determination to personal ability.

The aim of the revolution is to create increasing freedom for a constantly growing number of human beings. This revolution is essentially meant to be a permanent change; it cannot rest content with something transient.

Because of this, Marxism is accused of failing because it does not dare to submit what it has achieved to the critique of a new revolution (with the exception of the cultural revolution in China). No revolution can limit itself to a few countries: it has to operate throughout the world. Nor can it be the privilege of a particular generation or social class.

The capacity which allows man to achieve new freedom depends initially on his ability to separate nature from culture. Modern man no longer sees nature as a hostile force that is trying obstinately to escape from his control. He knows that he can

---

by the pharisaical bourgeois morality which followed on the French Revolution and left its traces in the civil legislation of many States. Until after Rubens and Tiepolo the arts ensured a place for the erotic element in churches; from the nineteenth century on, this element is no longer tolerated in religious buildings: this wholly corresponds to the line pursued by thinkers such as Diderot and Kant during the Enlightenment (P. Gorsen, *Das Prinzip Obszön. Kunst, Pornographie, Gesellschaft*, Hamburg, 1969, pp. 102–5). The liberating and redeeming aspects of sex have been brought out for the first time among Catholics by Marc Oraison, *Vie chrétienne et problèmes de la sexualité* (Paris, 1952), which was put on the Index. To see how far the taboo has been lifted in this matter, see F. J. Heggen, *Gezonde sexualiteit* (Roermond, 1967) and the special issue of *Lumière et Vie* (1970) on sexuality.
    [5] See the comments of A. Plack on Adorno and Mitscherlich ("Frau-Familie-Gesellschaft"), in *Kursbuch*, 17 (1969); K. Derksen, "Evangelie en culturele revolutie", in *Wending*, 24, 9 (Nov. 1969), pp. 566–76.

dominate nature and force it to assist him in the various areas in which he decides to win his own freedom.[6]

This applies also to the "sexual revolution"—a process which operates more freely because of the permissiveness of certain cultures. Sexuality today is separated from nature. This sexual culture is no longer seen as confined to the limits imposed by nature (fertility, procreation). It has become part of that wider determination of man to be free in order to be more fully himself. This allows man to reject the manipulation of sex by society and its one-sided institutionalization.[7]

This process brings with it the collapse of time-honoured taboos. The whole field of sexuality is now made public in such a way that it seems to be set free for good from the kind of prohibition which made sex clandestine as soon as it went beyond certain limits. Paul Balvet rightly speaks of the "end of the secretiveness"[8] which beset sexuality. Our age is rediscovering the world of sex. There may occasionally be a lack of sense of proportion, but at least sex is faced frankly as it is lived and made meaningful.

This rediscovery helps us to look for positive results, once we are beyond the initial stage. A large amount of the writing on sex is marked by a desire to explain and draw practical conclusions from this new understanding.

Guided by the data in the literature it seems possible to examine sexuality as a new dimension of our humanization, and to put it on the level where freedom can be exercised responsibly. We shall develop this approach in six stages.

First, we shall examine sexuality as an enigma, something that puts man in a state of wonder and unrest; secondly, the integration of sex into the whole nexus of human relationships so that it can be seen in the light of man's social conditions and therefore in terms of other people—for this gives it its human aspect; thirdly, some negative and positive aspects of modern sexuality

[6] K. Rahner, "Experiment Mensch—Theologisches über die Selbstmanipulation des Menschen", in *Schriften zur Theologie*, VIII (Einsiedeln, 1967), pp. 260–85; H. L. Parsons, "Mensch, Natur, Wert und Religion", in *Intern. Dialog Zeitschr.*, 2, 1 (1969), pp. 35–60.

[7] *Sex and Morality*, Report of the British Council of Churches, 1967; H. Ringeling, *Theologie und Sexualität* (Gütersloh, 1969), pp. 182–209.

[8] P. Balvet, "Fin d'une clandestinité", in *Eprit*, 11 (1960), pp. 1866–71.

and the revolution it is undergoing, together with certain new expressions or forms of sexual life; fourthly, the ethical meaning of modern sexuality; fifthly, the reaction of contemporary theology to the various questions raised by sexuality today; lastly, we shall offer some conclusions with regard to the future.

Sexuality as an Enigma

"The human being discovers and experiences his sexual condition as an enigma, and through this enigma he discovers the world of sex."[9] Human sexuality is grounded on desire. But underneath the actions which it sets in motion this desire is unspecified and unspecifiable; it is fascinated by the images which rouse it but incapable of resting there. Nourished on these images, sexual desire looks there in vain for the fulfilment of the confused promise which it bears within itself. This failure often leads to its degradation. This inability of desire to specify itself turns sex into something dense and opaque, with the result that sex remains, for a large part, imprisoned in an obscure and subterranean sphere.[10]

And so, as desire, sexuality is not definite; thanks to the body, it leads a chameleon-like existence and moves on the level of the imaginary. And "it is precisely because, in imagination, it puts itself forward in terms of *being*, of *existence*, that it becomes, right at the start, a lure or enticement".[11]

Consequently, sexuality presents itself as a phenomenon which is both attached to the rest of human life and outside it, straying apart from it in so far as it escapes man's consciousness. Closely tied up with pleasure, which turns it into something centrifugal, egotistical and narcissistic, sexuality, when reduced to itself, is threatened with disintegration at the level of concrete existence, and is forced to find an alibi in a kind of magic which claims to be some cosmic life-force in the universe, a corruption of the sacred; Igor Stravinsky's "Rite of Spring" as interpreted by Maurice Béjart is a good example of this. Here we have the sexual element seen as vital, sacred and determinative.

Sexuality is also enigmatic because, as Paul Ricoeur observed,

[9] F. Chirpaz, "Dimensions de la sexualité", in *Etudes*, 3 (1969), p. 409.
[10] *Ibid*.
[11] P. Julien, "Le discours sur le corps", in *Etudes*, 3 (1969), p. 431.

it is alien to what constitutes man as man, that is to say, to language, the tool and the institution.[12] From this point of view, sexuality is based on something which is both below and above the meaningful (*sur un pré-sens et sur un sur-sens*), and which does not depend on freedom or on its options. Thus the fascination of sex.

Such alienation often tempts man to break away from this force, with the result that he yields to licence. But licence also derives unconsciously from the kind of panic created by the repressed fear of death and evil: "Such liberation practically always leads to blasphemy and defiance; sexuality then becomes alienated in restless attitudes of specious subtlety and diabolism, and Eros becomes the servant of the dark god Thanatos."[13]

Then the sexual act confronts man with his body, which seems to him an enigma of shame. We may try to "spiritualize" sex as much as we like but we shall never be able to ignore its specific character. The sexual act is allied with defecation, and "like defecation it is difficult to detach it from a certain sense of shame, and it seeks to hide itself".[14] This is why physical love, even in marriage, eschews the light of day. The spirit seems to be disconcerted by the grossness of the sexual act, so much so that one can talk about "the metaphysical shame of the spirit confronted with *its* bestiality".[15] As Hesnard has pointed out, there is a sort of latency about sex which expresses itself in the wish to ignore it and a reluctance to talk about it.[16]

The enigma, then, tends to enclose itself in itself. But then we are reluctant to treat it as an object of thought; we run the risk of keeping it in the dark, and so of subjecting ourselves passively to it like animals. When man "does not take charge of his sexuality (and he does not do this by preventing his mind from penetrating into that field) he becomes desperate, and paradoxically retreats into purely animal pleasures".[17]

[12] P. Ricoeur, "La merveille, l'errance, l'énigme", in *Esprit*, 11 (1960), p. 1675.
[13] J. Brun, "Aliénation et sexualité", in *Esprit*, 11 (1960), p. 1810.
[14] J. Sarano, "L'esprit, le sexe et la bête", in *Esprit*, 11 (1960), p. 1850.
[15] *Id.*, p. 1851.
[16] A. Hesnard, "Note sur la méconnaissance sexuelle courante", in *Esprit*, 11 (1960), pp. 1864–6.
[17] P. Balvet, *op. cit.*, p. 1867.

Many psychoanalysts emphasize this concern with the humanization of the unconscious, and therefore, of sexuality. Nacht says: "Today we are less worried about the meanderings of the unconscious as such and more with the relations between the unconscious and the ego in so far as we can comprehend them."[18] Erich Fromm shows the same concern. He tried to compare the teachings of Freud with those of Marx in order to find psychoanalytical solutions to the problem of sexual and social alienation.[19]

The Sexual and the Social

The extension of the individual organism into the environment compels the individual to seek full integration there, and to reach beyond himself. This is so even if we only consider the couple whose physiological and emotional equilibrium implies "a mutual adjustment between individual automatic elements".[20] This means that, at that level of communication with the environment, sex is experienced as a living and organized system which "is also evidence of and ensures a permanent location in the world".[21]

When sex emerges in the consciousness as a desire born of the unconscious, it qualifies man's sense of being in the world. It establishes itself in man's existence and imposes a new life-style, an orientation towards the other person, combined with a tendency towards life lived together: the result is an interpersonal relationship.

This is why Marc Oraison observed that "normality coincides with the *psychological possibility* of interpersonal relationship".[22] And this, according to Ricoeur, presupposes an emergence of the person at the sexual level in the form of tenderness or gentleness, which is "an attempt to re-establish a symbol of innocence, a

---

[18] S. Nacht, *La présence du psychanalyste* (Paris, 1963), p. 1.
[19] E. Fromm, *The Art of Loving* (New York, 1960); *Beyond the Chains of Illusion* (New York, 1963); *Marx's Concept of Man* (New York, 1961).
[20] M. de Ceccaty, "Essai d'énoncé biologique", in *Esprit*, 11 (1960), p. 1720.
[21] C. H. Nodet, "Sexualité en situation", in *Esprit*, 11 (1960), p. 1753.
[22] M. Oraison, "Enquête", in *Esprit*, 11 (1960), p. 1841.

ritualization of our dream of innocence, and a restoration of integrity and the integration of the flesh".[23]

In contrast with eroticism, which only cares for pleasure when left to itself, tenderness is inspired by the desire for a link between persons which lasts, becomes more intense and more intimate. Thanks to this, "the relation to the other prevails and can enlist the erotic element as the sensual component of sexuality".[24]

Since it cannot exist outside mutual commitment, tenderness is the freedom which gives rise to love—the lasting embodiment of the intent to create and maintain the encounter. As a result, tenderness is a value which re-evaluates sexuality and makes it possible to sublimate it at the level of celibacy, particularly when it corresponds to a deliberate commitment to the world. It can even do so at the level of homosexual relationships.

As the means of mutual communication between souls in their bodies, tenderness cannot be separated from a richly structured relationship which is capable of braving the enigma of sexuality, through the mutual admission and recognition of a secret wound of which it softens both the pain and the shame. It is at this point that sexuality is endowed with its full human meaning, and makes a powerful contribution to the humanization of man: love culminates in friendship.

Once poured into the social current, sexuality sheds what it contained of animal sexuality. As Thibon has rightly pointed out, this is a genuine sublimation, brought about by a shift of values. The social element restrains the tyrannical appetites of sex. It prevents the individual from locking himself up in the prison of his egotistic self. It enlists in the service of society a thousand psychological elements (images, feelings, desires) that are sexually neutral, but which sex always tends to monopolize for itself.[25]

Much the same point of view is held by Scheler who, beyond this, sees in the restraint of man's libidinous instincts the very means of achieving freedom. This limitation allows psychic energy to transform itself into sexual sympathy.[26]

[23] P. Ricoeur, op. cit., p. 1669.
[24] Id., p. 1671; cf. T. Lemaire's excellent book, De tederheid (2nd edn., Utrecht, 1968).
[25] G. Thibon, La crise moderne de l'amour (Paris, 1953).
[26] M. Scheler, "Über Scham und Schamgefühl", in Zur Ethik und Erkenntnislehre, Schriften aus dem Nachlasse (Berlin, 1933).

The importance of this social element for sexuality has been emphasized by Buerger-Prinz. Among the three components of sex—the biological-instinctive, the sociological and the cultural factors—he assigns first place to the sociological factor on the ground that anomaly and perversion always originate in a primary sexual unsociability.[27] The sexual instinct implies a demand for identification which only the social dimension can stabilize and humanize.

Modern Sexuality

In Stendhal we can already find a view of sex which foreshadows the understanding of our age: the fulfilment of individual desires freed from the constraints of society.[28] But it was no doubt Gehlen who, fifteen years ago, was the first to analyse the sexual situation and to forecast what has happened since.

According to him, the sexual explosion is rooted in the breakdown of religious, social and political barriers. The waning of the influence of institutions brought with it a breakdown in the social habits providing the recoil needed for the exercise of sexual responsibility. On the other hand, the questioning of accepted values made modern man fall back on himself but deprived him of the possibility of examining his own consciousness and mastering the vast field of psychological differentiation.

From this point of view, the instability of the inner world finds its parallel in that of the outer world.[29] In this context, "love, as the subject of fiction, . . . the demand of natural law to have one's own feelings, has been transformed . . . into a natural element, so to speak, of our civilization".[30] Private life is put before marriage and family, and narcissism is on the increase: "The process of the analytical interpretation of love and sex, and the difficulty of standing outside oneself and looking at oneself objectively, have continued to grow. They have culminated in a pan-sexual image

[27] H. Buerger-Prinz, "Psychopathologie der Sexualität", in *Die Sexualität des Menschen*, 5 (1955).
[28] Stendhal (H. Beyle), *De l'amour*.
[29] A. Gehlen, "Über die Geburt der Freiheit aus der Entfremdung", in *Archiv. f. Rechts und Sozialphilosophie*, XL (1953); *id.*, *Macht einmal anders gesehen* (Zürich, 1954).
[30] H. Schelsky, *Soziologie der Sexualität* (5th edn., Hamburg, 1956).

of man, based on a popularized theory of the libido and Kinsey's statistics of orgasm in society."[31]

This loss of the meaning of sexuality and love today has been analysed with particular import by Paul Ricoeur. He sees it as distinguished by three basic features.

The decline into insignificance: the laxity which followed the lifting of sexual taboos, the mixing of the sexes, their equality, and the spreading of sexological literature among the public have helped to reduce sex to a biological function without mystery. Thus sex has become so de-personalized as to become anonymous. The psychoanalysts say that their clients "increasingly complain of the fact that they are incapable of experiencing the affective involvement of their whole personality in the act of intercourse, and that they make love without loving".[32]

Exacerbation: today the meaning of sexuality tends to be merely a kind of compensation for the disappointments created by the upheavals and changes in society, and becomes constantly more demanding: "Eroticism becomes one way of spending one's leisure, and often it is the cheapest kind of leisure, at least when it is a matter of crude eroticism."[33] To keep sex interesting, one has to practise it to the point of becoming its slave.

Absurdity: "Lastly, at a deeper level, eroticism is the expression of a more radical disappointment, the disappointment about the meaning of things. When there is no more meaning to anything, the only thing that remains is instant pleasure and all its contrivances."[34] When incoherent, sexuality has no longer any human meaning and becomes a mere trifling. This then leads to a barefaced commercialization of sex (posters, illustrated magazines, films, pornographic literature), which has provoked protest in the United States. Paradoxically, this titillation leads to paroxysm.

To define modern sexuality exclusively in terms of what has just been said would be to over-simplify matters, because the preceding analysis stressed the negative side without the positive elements that would restore the balance. The modern rejection of tradition and of institutions means, in a positive sense, the rejection of the alienation created by these two factors.

[31] *Ibid*.
[32] P. Ricoeur, *op. cit.*, p. 1672.
[33] *Id.*, p. 1673.
[34] *Ibid*.

In many parts of the world this positive rejection has become revolutionary. It attacks the social injustice and the inhuman accumulation of material comfort in certain forms of capitalism, the oppressive and anonymous powers and structures of a hier-archical bureaucracy, and the cancer-like growth of a society which has no other aim than to proliferate itself indefinitely.[35]

Many people today have realized that man must be humanized in order to transform society in depth, and that this has to be done in a struggle and protest which reveal man's true ambitions and potential; in an educative process affecting the mental and psychological structures; in freedom of speech; and in thinking more in terms of being than in terms of having.[36]

We can distinguish two situations in modern sexuality: one which rejects alienation by plunging into aberrations and licence, without accepting the struggle such a rejection demands; and another, which fights alienation in revolutionary terms and seeks to create a radical change in life: "The change that is required is not merely concerned with the relation between the sexes, the juridical and political equality of both sexes in their contractual or simply assumed relationships, and the de-feudalization of the relations between the sexes. The transformation must affect all the relations (emotional and ideological) between sex and society."[37]

The control of sexual life lies not with institutions, but with those who are involved, and this control must operate in the direction of the humanization of happiness.

The body must recover its full meaning in order to restore the balance of the human condition. Here modern man has shaken off the shackles of Manicheism by endowing the body with a sacred meaning which humanizes it: "Today the sacred has penetrated into man's private life, and this has given our human relationships their fullness of meaning and their dramatic

[35] P. Ricoeur, "Réforme et révolution dans l'Université", in *Eprit*, 6 (1968), pp. 987–1002.

[36] J. Julliard, "Syndicalisme révolutionnaire et révolution étudiante", in *Esprit*, 6 (1968), pp. 1037–45; H. Giese and G. Schmidt, *Studentensexuali-tät* (Hamburg, 1968); "Education", in *Time* (30 May 1969), p. 43.

[37] H. Lefebvre, *La vie quotidienne dans le monde moderne* (Paris, 1968), p. 373.

character. This aspect actually bestows on sexuality its tragic seriousness." [38]

More than his predecessors modern man feels the need to show himself as he is. Here the expression of sexuality is no longer a problem. We have become accustomed, as Georges Bataille required, no longer to worry about indecency, and to call each element of sex by its proper name. The whole field of sex now lies clearly exposed and free from darkness and anxiety.

Until the end of the nineteenth century there was no literature about sexuality. The breakthrough came with psychiatry, particularly with the publication of Krafft-Ebing's *Psychopathologia sexualis* (1840–1902). "Then, with Freud, the various neuroses began to be studied. With him and his followers the field of normal sexuality became the object of scientific study. The term 'sexology' is not pedantry; its use marked the time when the study of sexuality became a science." [39]

This was what Freud intended. For him the refusal to face sexuality explicitly was a threat to the freedom and spiritual growth of groups and individuals alike. As Hesnard says: "The very fact that man can dominate his sexuality is the truth which triumphs over all mystification." [40]

If the fate of man is determined by everyday happenings, this is because his life itself is a drama, created by the tension between life and death, and failure and success—a tension man experiences as man. In this drama, which is identical with the human adventure, the sexual element henceforth plays a clear and leading part for the evaluation of everyday trivialities, for this evaluation is the only means of rescuing its various aspects from anonymity and of interpreting the signs of the times.

Hence we have new sexual experiences, inspired by the concern for free giving and authenticity. This implies a search for certainty in co-existence, a plurality of meaning, an appreciation of the sexual ritual, and care to avoid repetitiveness and not to let the future be fixed in inhuman structures.

Here we are thinking particularly of the "communes" and the

[38] P. Müller, "Enquête", in *Esprit*, 11 (1960), p. 1708.
[39] P. Balvet, *op. cit.*, p. 1868.
[40] A. Hesnard, *op. cit.*, p. 1866.

"living theatre".[41] In both cases the sexual element is meant to counteract alienation and to be a means of vital association at the social level. It is not primarily pursued for the sake of pleasure, but in order to encounter the Other in others, and this as a means of initiation, and the discovery, experienced together, of the depths of human existence. This kind of sexuality is possessive without acquisitiveness, free from mystifying taboos, controlling and no longer controlled.

It would be too simple and unfair to look on those experiences as particular forms of degeneracy and perversion, or to condemn them morally without appeal. On the contrary, we not only must note them without prejudice, but we must try to understand the message for the future which lies behind such extremes.

Modern Sexuality and Ethics

That modern man is now free from conventions and sexual taboos does not necessarily mean that he is adjusted to his sexuality. This involves in practice too many subjective and objective exciting elements which are difficult to control and channel. But what do we substitute for the institutions which provided some criteria for this adjustment—limited but easy to apply?

"Social engineering" (the application of modern psychological techniques) is a supposed replacement: "psychotherapy and psychological treatment, sexual education, marriage guidance, birth-control and child-guidance clinics, the education of groups and human relations",[42] try to substitute a clear self-awareness and a concrete judgment of reality for abstract and outdated moral laws.

Unfortunately, in order to be practical, psychology had to be made popular; in doing this it limited itself to the most superficial aspects of human conduct. This was inevitable since it intended to take over the tasks left behind by institutions and rules. By the same token it had to become conventional, and this diminished its scientific value precisely at a time when its social function became more important.

This adjustment of man to his sexuality cannot work without

[41] E. Billeter, *Living Theatre—Paradise Now* (Hilversum, 1968). Cf. note 60.
[42] H. Schelsky, *op. cit.*, pp. 198-9.

an ethics. His sexual impulses cannot be severed from the fact that they are aimed at another: "The sexual element implies the search for another person as a goal. It must be seen in the light of this bi-polar relationship between the ego, the self and the other."[43]

This fact has ethical consequences, because ethics is primarily concerned with relations with others. Moreover, it is possible that the relation of ethics to sexuality is such that the first constitutes the sublimation of the second: "the product and strategy of that struggle which goes on inside ourselves between the instinct of survival and the instinct of death throughout the vicissitudes of emotions that are always ambivalent".[44]

But if sexuality postulates an ethics, the fact that we are dealing with modern sexuality prevents us from appealing to an ethics of the past, an ethics of the essentialist type. Today's society demands a new kind of integration and regulation of sexuality.

The possibilities opened up by the disappearance of the clandestine character of sex run the danger of contortion if sexual ethics were not to discover a new sacred form of sexuality, in order to give it a positive form and restore its symbolism. Such an ethics must provide sex with the means to see itself simultaneously as the expression of man in his relationship to the absolute, and as giving expression to those depths of man's existence where the bonds between persons are formed.

The religious renewal which marks our age is certainly capable of creating a concrete, significant and modern sexual ethics. For this renewal contains a revaluation of the mystical and unifying dimension of interpersonal love, and so can become a source of light for the humanization of sexuality and love.[45]

Finally, this new ethics of sexuality must be based on responsibility, which is the principle of social identification, and without which sex becomes merely an erratic pursuit of pleasure. This is why it cannot be based on suasions outside responsible commitment. For modern man the "only acceptable ethics is that which aims at what is implied in sexual behaviour and tries to express

[43] F. Chirpaz, "L'intention de rencontre", in *Esprit*, 11 (1960), p. 1834.
[44] M. Dufrenne, "Mythe, science et éthique du sexe", in *Esprit*, 11 (1960), p. 1709.
[45] De Lestapis, "Enquête", in *Esprit*, 11 (1960), p. 1697.

itself there, namely, the quest for the other, for communing with the other in the whole of his being";[46] and this implies a fully accepted mutual responsibility.

The Theological Approach to the Humanization of Sexuality

In recent years, both Churches and theologians have been increasingly concerned with matters related to sexuality. There is a vast and still increasing literature which deals with divorce, birth control, woman, celibacy, homosexuality, and so on. In the most recent studies the emphasis has shifted towards adaptation to the human sciences concerned and towards dialogue with these disciplines. One may speak of a general toning-down of the norms that governed sexual life.[47]

One may wonder whether theological discussion is at present not too exclusively focused on marriage as an institution, and on the norms that derive from it. The assumption that love relationships belong exclusively to marriage is being questioned.[48]

Historical research has shown that the institutionalization of marriage and the severe rules for sexual behaviour, often put forward as Christian norms and as based on natural law, are in fact the norms that developed in the bourgeois society that arose between the sixteenth and nineteenth centuries. Universal validity has been claimed for those norms.

The Churches and their theology showed a certain affinity with those norms because of Augustinian influences, and this is why they helped to spread them (for instance, the condemnation of masturbation).[49] It is a pity that today we have lost sight of the historical origin of the sexual problem.

Interest in the question of how man realizes himself within a given institution is declining; it is turning increasingly towards the question of how man can be set free in order to become fully conscious of his humanity. Hence two questions: how can man

[46] F. Chirpaz, *op. cit.*, p. 1838.
[47] J. Messner, "Ehemoral und Entscheidungsethik", in *Hochland*, 62 (Jan./Feb. 1970), pp. 1–19.
[48] G. Sartory-Reidick, "Kan die Katholische Kirche die Ehescheidung dulden?", in *Ehe*, 6 (1969/2), pp. 49–66, with bibliography.
[49] J. M. W. van Ussel, *Geschiedenis van het seksuele probleem* (Meppel, 1968), esp. pp. 78–82; D. S. Bailey, *The Man-Woman Relation in Christian Thought* (London, 1959); H. Ringeling, *op. cit.*, pp. 9–141.

live his sexuality in an authentic manner, and how does he subject himself to the alienation of false gods and worshipping them?

Harvey Cox has devoted a chapter to the theme of "Sex and Secularization".[50] In urban Western culture man has shed the old structures that dominated his behaviour, but, lacking a system of values, has landed in a vacuum. The mass media fill this vacuum with new codes of conduct. They have created new idols, which, through commercial exploitation, have destroyed human freedom with their tyranny. "Nowhere is the humanization of life more frustrated. Nowhere is a clear word of exorcism more needed."[51]

He illustrates this by referring to the "playboy" and Miss America, who play the same part as Adonis and Aphrodite did in pagan society.[52] Catholicism has acquired some elements of this phenomenon in the cult of Mary. He also maintains that precisely the Protestantism which rejected the cult of Mary has encouraged this idolatry.

His argument in no sense derives from a negative attitude towards sex, but is rather a protest against the *cult* of sex.[53] It is for that reason that he makes his own the prophetic protest against fertility rites in the Old Testament.

The projection of a Miss America as the ideal woman creates false values and, because of this uniformity of presentation, prevents the growth of pluriformity through individual development which should lead to conscious identification. This idolatry offends God in his divinity because God is "the centre and source of value".[54]

An evangelical concept of sexuality implies that it be not confused with unrealistic romantic love or mere pleasure, as is done, for instance, in the magazine *Playboy*. This would take all human meaning out of sexuality.[55] But when we combine the Bible with modern civilization we may reach new forms of sexuality which may help man to develop a greater sense of responsibility.

Ringeling has studied "Theology and Sexuality" in detail, both

[50] Harvey Cox, *The Secular City* (London, SCM edn., 1967).
[51] *Id.*, p. 194.
[52] *Id.*, pp. 195 f.; but see also the protest of "The new feminists: revolt against 'sexism' ", in *Time* (21 Nov. 1969), pp. 39–43.
[53] H. Cox, *op. cit.*, p. 199.
[54] *Id.*, p. 199.   [55] *Id.*, p. 204.

historically and theoretically.[56] Very different in this from Barth and Thielicke, for instance, he starts from the social aspect and does not oppose person to society. He tries to build up a Christian ethics on the basis of subjectivity. It is a pity that his theological vision of sexuality is much less solid than his sociological one, which is far more penetrating.

The Ecumenist has tried to open up an ecumenical dialogue on the subject: "Sexuality on the island, called earth".[57] Here Gregory Baum tries to put sexuality in the light of God's plan for man, and to show that in sex God offers man a new aspect of humanization. Human life is oriented towards development and increasing reconciliation for the sake of the community.[58] Baum nevertheless strictly maintains the ambiguity of sex; sex can express itself in love and tenderness as well as in hostility and the lust for power. Today it is no longer possible to impose the traditional norms on sexual life, but we must firmly hold on to Christian teaching about the meaning of human life when we try to explain sexuality.

New perspectives have been opened up in Holland, in the first issue of *Speling* (1969):[59] these are important for a new Christian approach to matters of sex. It is devoted to the subject of "Woman and the Priest". It gives a positive evaluation of the sexual element in the relationship between the celibate and women. The second issue of *Tegenspraak* has an article on "Community and Commune" where the subject is approached from the angle of a critique of society. It looks for new forms of sexuality in the direction of a growing humanism.[60]

Conclusion

What has been said so far shows how far the theological approach is from the philosophical and anthropological one. The

[56] H. Ringeling, *op. cit.*; cf. the discussion of the literature in G. Hummel.

[57] The first article was written by two Christian Brothers, D. Darst and J. Forgue, in *The Ecumenist*, 7, 6 (1969), pp. 81-7; J. M. Gustafson replied for the Protestants, pp. 87-9, and G. Baum for the Catholics, pp. 90-2.

[58] G. Baum, *art. cit.*, p. 91.

[59] *Speling* has taken the place of the Carmelite review, *Carmel*.

[60] Cf. B. Wilhelmer, "Kommune", in *Tegenspraak*, 2 (1969/70), pp. 44-55; F. Florin and S. Theunis, "Tussen kommuniteit en kommune", *ibid.*, pp. 56-60.

theologians have only begun to survey the terrain and are trying to catch up. They proceed on two lines: ethical in the broad sense of the word, and strictly theological.

1. In Christian ethics they try to integrate sexuality fully into the process of humanization. Sexuality can no longer be treated exclusively in the context of teaching about marriage. We have to learn to speak more positively about the various aspects of sex, for instance, about "tenderness".[61] On the other hand, we shall have to protest against both the distortion of sex at the purely individual level, and against its commercial exploitation and its "repressive de-sublimation" by the social structures of the Western world.[62] Groups represented by such publications as *Kritischer Katholizismus* and *Tegenspraak* are already working on these lines. Somehow, a prophetic attitude that can distinguish between pharisaism and sexual voodoo is a basic requirement.

2. It will also be necessary to re-integrate the sexual element in theological studies. The biblical, or rather, Pauline image of the Church uses the physical union of husband and wife to symbolize the relation between Christ and his Church. The mystics have always lived and expressed the affinity which exists between their experiences and sex. Sexual relationship must again become the image and example of all relationships in the Church.[63] This factor could be carried over into ecclesiology, liturgy, the teaching on the sacraments, and so on. Then, perhaps, theological language will no longer be sterile, but meaningful once more.

[61] Teilhard was a pioneer here because he was aware of the fact that the meaning of sexuality extends beyond procreation, education, marital faithfulness and social practices; cf. É. Rideau, "La sexualité selon Teilhard de Chardin", in *Nouv. Rev. Théol.*, 100 (1968), pp. 173–90. The aspect of redemption must become clear in sexuality.

[62] H. Marcuse, *Eros and Civilization*.

[63] A. Greeley, *op. cit.*

Eugene TeSelle

AUGUSTINE
THE THEOLOGIAN

This totally modern critique considers Augustine's entire theological achievement not according to the rubrics of systematic theology but along the creative lines with which Augustine himself was concerned. TeSelle has uncovered the framework of Augustine's thought with unusual clarity, and is the first scholar to offer an in-depth study of the crucial period 400–407 in Augustine's life. $12.50

David Tracy

THE ACHIEVEMENT
OF BERNARD LONERGAN

Professor Tracy of the University of Chicago Divinity School analyzes the historical development and contemporary significance of Bernard Lonergan, from his rediscovery of the significance of the scientific exigence in the theology of St. Thomas Aquinas through his discovery of the shift toward the critical in philosophy. "David Tracy has done a delicate job in describing briefly the complicated intellectual contexts of Lonergan's development. Probably no one could have done it so well — a masterful job of exposition." — *Michael Novak.* $9.50

Donald P. Gray

THE ONE AND THE MANY
Teilhard de Chardin's
Vision of Unity

This vital contribution to Teilhardian studies explores the early essays, elucidating the French Jesuit's concept of the eschatological communion of the many, an idea the author sees at the heart of Teilhard's view of unity. In *The One and the Many* Gray succeeds in creating a remarkable synthesis of the overriding concerns and themes that mark the writing and life of Teilhard. $6.95

Joseph Donceel, Editor

THE MARECHAL READER

A wide and representative sample of the thought of the man who introduced the transcendental method into Thomist philosophy. "Those who have wrestled with Maréchal themselves or who have endeavored to present his thought to others cannot fail to appreciate the accuracy and clarity of his presentation. We have here the heart of Maréchal." — *Gerald McCool.* $6.95

J. Edgar Bruns

THE ART AND THOUGHT
OF JOHN

Father Bruns, chairman of the Graduate Department of Theology at St. Michael's College, University of Toronto, explores John's artistry and its relation to the intellectual and philosophical world around him. His analysis and comparisons of the Johannine forms illuminate the rich originality of development, and consistency of John's theology and writing. "A useful and enlightening guide for the educated Christian who seeks a more profound acquaintance with this most 'Spiritual Gospel.' " — *David M. Stanley, S.J.* $4.95

Karl Rahner

THE TRINITY

In this unique study of Trinitarian Doctrine Rahner investigates two treatises of the Church, "On the One God" and "On the Triune God" and sheds new light upon the question of the relation and distinction between these two treatises. He analyzes the Trinity as an absolute Mystery, presents a systematic summary of the official Trinitarian Doctrine, and discusses the consequences of a deeper understanding of the Trinity. $4.95

HERDER AND HERDER

232 Madison Avenue, New York, N.Y. 10016

continuum

the magazine that speaks for itself

Continuum is an independent quarterly sponsored by the Saint Xavier College, Chicago, edited by Justus George Lawler in association with Gregory Baum, Daniel Berrigan, Leslie Dewart, Gabriel Moran, Rosemary Ruether, George Tavard, and others. It contains vital, relevant, enlightened, contemporary theological writing and penetrating commentary on today's church and non-church worlds.

Indicative of the great range of thought coming from CONTINUUM's contributors are articles from recent issues, among them: Thomas Anderson on revolution in Central America; Gabriel Moran on the role of the adult in religious education; Leo J. O'Donovan on Bernard Lonergan; Raymond Benoit on Teilhard as Alchemist; and Leslie Dewart on Transcendental Thomism; and a memoriam issue on Thomas Merton that featured a brilliant array of tribute and analytical writings. Themes for the 1970 issues include: Eschatology and Utopia; Critical Social Theory and the Frankfurt School; The Body; and The New Left: Theory and Interest. Contributors to the controversial year-opening issue will include, among many, Roland E. Murphy, Robert L. Shinn, Kenneth Rexroth and Herbert Aptheker.

Subscriptions available through:
Herder and Herder
232 Madison Avenue
New York, N.Y. 10016